How to Sell a Business

The #1 Guide to Maximising Your Company Value and Achieving a Quick Sale

Joanna Miller

First Edition

ISBN: 978-1494367695

For my mother, my hero

Contents

Introduction

In order to maximise your business exit, it is worth knowing as much as possible about the sale process, ideally before you start, so that you can not only increase your chances of crossing the finish line, but also get the maximum pay-out possible.

Looking back at my experience of selling my first business, I was rather naive. I bumbled along, hitting all sorts of obstacles, which could have been avoided if I had this book. I discovered selling a business is a science and an art—both of which can be studied, but it doesn't stop there. You also have to have the strength of an ox, patience of a saint, and craftiness of a fox!

This book has been created for owner-managers that have decided to sell their business (and exit) or employees that have been asked to prepare the business for sale, who want the inside story on how to increase the likelihood of success.

Whether you're just starting to contemplate a sale, or are half way through the process, this book will help you to:

- Gain techniques and tips on how to personally best maximise your profit
- Demystify the business sale process so that you can be one step ahead of the buyer
- Be prepared to handle the emotional journey
- Increase the likelihood that you sell the first time through the sale process
- Ensure the sale process goes as quickly and smoothly as possible

- Understand your current valuation and how to best increase it
- Avoid 'price chipping' (the buyer reducing the offer price) and costly mistakes
- Escape an earn out (having to stay on as an employee and hit targets after the sale)
- Ultimately create a successful exit strategy so that you can start a new adventure, enjoy more time with loved ones, spend some of your hard-earned cash, and do all the things you've always wanted to do but never had time

Perhaps you're an owner/manager interested in selling because it's time to retire, or you're ready for a new adventure. Or maybe you're an employee instructed to sell by your shareholders. You might be just starting out, or half way through the process. Either way, this book will help you on your journey. Furthermore, this book will assist owner-mangers or employees from any industry, whether you're managing a local coffee shop, a national software house, or an international manufacturing plant.

Just as no two businesses are the same, selling your business will be a unique experience. This book is by no means 'the right and only way' to sell a business; however, what it does do is prepare you for the journey, provides practical information, offers invaluable tips to make the process faster, smoother, and more cost effective, in addition to demonstrating how to avoid pitfalls.

Unfortunately, this book doesn't come with a guarantee that by the end of reading this book you will definitely sell your business, but it will definitely increase your chances.

How to Sell a Business: The #1 Guide to Maximising Your Company Value and Achieving a Quick Business Sale is structured as if you were starting at the beginning, which is to prepare for sale, and takes you right through to the end point, where the cash is in your bank account. No matter where you are in your sale process, I recommend you read this book from start to finish. Just speed read it through and then go back and focus on the particular part of the journey that you're currently on.

Part One is about checking your reasoning behind wanting to sell. Before placing your company officially on the market, it's best to get your company in order to maximise its valuation, which is what Part Two is about. Part Three is making sure you have the right business sale team in place. Part Four is about going to market and sealing the deal. Part Five covers a number of practical tips on various stages along the way, to make sure you are prepared and informed for everything.

Enjoy the journey to success!

Part One – To Sell or Not to Sell?

The Sale Process Stages

Most businesses are for sale if the price is right. When someone asks, 'Is your business for sale?' I recommend you say yes. It doesn't cost you anything, and it keeps the opportunity open for further exploration.

Exploring opportunities is one thing; entering into the business sale process is another. You definitely don't want to go into it lightly. The process is costly and mentally and physically draining. It's not an activity to enter half-heartedly by either the seller or the buyer. A high level of commitment is necessary from all parties.

The actual sale process may be longer than you think, and it involves a number of stages in order to maximise your valuation. The stages are as follows:

- Making the decision to sell
- Preparing your business for sale
- Getting the right business sale team in place
- Going to market to find a buyer
- Carrying out successful due diligence
- Completion Day and the after-party
- Communicating the successful sale to the market

When is the best time to sell

In an ideal world, the best time to sell is when your business is on the up-and-up, still growing with a strong order book, running efficiently, managed effectively, and the going is good. The trick is to recognise this point as it approaches, and make the most of the window of opportunity when it arrives. My business partner and I always looked out for this window, and our indicators were our scarcity in the market, the number of clients with which we had contracts, the volume we were processing, and forecasting over the next few years. Even though we recognised the window of opportunity when it came along, we were a little late. This was partly because the business was going really well and everyone was enjoying themselves, and partly because our business sale process took longer than we expected.

The indicators for your business are likely to be different, taking a number of different factors into account, such as scarcity of your product and services in the market, the market size, future opportunity, profit margins (are they growing or shrinking?), and where your business is in the market cycle. It could even be that you have gone to see some venture capitalist (VC) companies who told you that you need a larger order book.

TIP: To make sure you don't miss the boat, define the indicators to look out for, which show when the best time to sell is approaching. Make sure this is checked regularly, so have it as an agenda item at your board meetings.

If you are in a market cycle that doesn't have a 'best time to sell' period coming up for the foreseeable future, it could still be the perfect time to sell. Just remember to choose your 'ready to sale' point very carefully by taking the calendar into consideration (more details in Part Five—When should we go out to market?).

Why do people want to sell

Here are a number of reasons why someone would want to sell their business:

- To cash in on their investment to get the castle, fast car, big yacht, or private aeroplane
- To take advantage of ripe market conditions
- To respond to a request to sell from a potential buyer
- To pursue a different venture
- To avoid a foreseeable future downturn in the industry or market
- To increase the financial support to the business
- To provide personal development and growth opportunities that otherwise wouldn't exist
- To retire
- To find a more meaningful way to do business (loss of interest in current company)
- To get cash now! (distress sale)
- To better manage personal or health problems (i.e., death in the family, divorce, etc.)

I fully acknowledge that deciding on whether or not to sell will depend on your current financial position. A few million can be totally life changing for someone who has very low net worth, but if you already have assets of more than 10M you might choose not to sell as having the business is a form of diversification as part of your investment portfolio.

And some people make the decision to sell and then change their mind because:

- They realise they don't have the time to do what is necessary to make it happen
- The valuation that they can achieve in the current market isn't worth the effort
- There are things they can do in the medium term that will help increase the value. Perhaps the best plan now is to work on the business until it's in a better position to sell

How is a business actually sold

Hundreds of businesses are sold and bought every day. You'll generally find that newspapers cover the huge deals, and you'll hear through word-of-mouth about transactions in your industry, yet you won't hear about the vast majority of deals.

The sale of a business is normally brokered by corporate financiers. Corporate financiers can be one of the Big Four (KMPG, Ernest & Young, Deloitte, PwC) or a boutique company specialising in a particular industry or size of business (based on revenue). You will also find brokers online where you can list your business for sale on their website and may also help you close the deal with a prospective buyer.

The Business Sales Process in a Nutshell

In upcoming chapters I'll go in to quite a bit of detail about the sales process, but before we get there, let me give you a quick overview as to what happens.

Once your target buyer list is agreed, your broker will prepare a teaser letter and Memorandum of Information (MOI) document. The broker will distribute the teaser letter to the target buyer list and interested parties will express an interest by signing a non-disclosure agreement (NDA). The broker will then send out the Memorandum of Information. If the buyer remains interested, a meeting will be arranged with you and your sale team present; think of it as a first date. Once they've met with you, and if they are still interested, they will place an indicative offer in writing for you to consider.

With your advisor's help, you'll shortlist the prospective buyers and due diligence will start. Due diligence is where the buyer looks at your company in detail to make sure you are selling what they want to buy. Essentially, the buyer is looking for peace of mind that your offer will provide them with the end result they require. Now is the time to be truthful as everything will be scrutinised and come out in the wash.

To aid due diligence, a data room will be prepared which will contain all your available company documentation, covering all aspects of the business in electronic format.

During this time, the original indicative offers are firmed up and a potential buyer will push for exclusivity in order to show they are keen to complete the deal with you. If all goes well, you end up concluding the sale in the solicitors' offices and signing loads of paperwork. Once all the signatures are dried the deal is complete, it's time to celebrate!

Although it may seem straightforward, this process will take months, and in extreme cases even years, to accomplish.

Please keep in mind that the Sell Your Business Store is full of helpful templates, checklists and packs that have been created to assist you through the business sale journey. Check them out at:

http://www.SellYourBusiness.biz/store/

The Financial Cost of Selling

You might be wondering how much it costs to sell a business. However, there are more than just financial costs associated with selling. There's the cost of time, health, and the extra work the sale brings, all of which could affect the financial price tag, either by reducing it because you're spread too thin, or positively because you've prepared your business for sale extremely well and have lined up your ducks in a row.

There's no rule of thumb on costs, but a good estimation is 5% of your total valuation. Some advice is more expensive, especially if your company structure is complex and the structure of the deal is complicated. Here are the professional service areas where you will be spending to make sure the sale happens:

- Corporate financiers will help you broker the deal to get the best price and show off the financial numbers in the best possible light
- Accountants will prove to the potential buyers the statutory information is correct

- Solicitors will draw up all the legal documentation in order for the sale to be successfully completed
- Personal tax advisors will make sure you can easily compare different deals and what effect the numbers have with regards to your personal tax situation

The above 5% assumes you are successful in selling your business the first time round. However, do be aware that some deals fall through, and many of these fees are non-refundable. Going through the sales process twice may incur twice the cost, increasing your fees to 10% of valuation. And let's not forget the cost of your sanity too! That's why it's so important to understand the full process and be one step ahead rather than operating blindly.

What's involved in preparing for a sale

Selling a business is very similar to selling a home. Once you've found and instructed your broker, agreed a valuation, and had it advertised to the market, offers should start to come in. Thankfully you don't have to worry about chains!

Doing up the house before prospective buyers come and visit is exactly what needs to happen with a business. There is quite a lot of preparation, and the more time you spend on preparing for this, the easier it will be to sell your business. Preparation will reduce your stress and help you cope more easily with the questions asked by prospective buyers.

TIP: Think of selling your business like selling a house. Before you sell a house, you remove clutter, put on a fresh coat of paint, fix anything broken, and make it look as desirable as possible.

If you're wondering how long it takes to prepare a business for sale, just like a house, it all depends on how large the business is, the state you've kept it in, and how much of a hurry you are in. It may take you two to six months to prepare your business for sale. Effort is needed in all parts of the business and of course general business upkeep needs to happen during the sale process too.

What can happen during the sale

In a word, *anything* can happen during the sale, so be prepared and expect the unexpected. For example, some business owners think a sale will take years and yet it shifts in months. Others expect a sale after a third or fourth attempt only to realise success after six tries for completion. Or everything can seem perfect, and one hour before the deal is done the buyer gets cold feet and decides to walk away.

During the sale process, my business partner and I experienced a number of unexpected things. The original timeline was expected to be 12 months as suggested by our corporate financier, yet it turned out to be 22 months. Part of the delay was caused by having to change our corporate finance firm twice. Can you believe that our corporate financier changed jobs, and then went back to his original firm?!

Unexpectedly, we went around the business sale cycle a total of five times, had ten potential buyers at different times, and had four indicative price offers in which the highest price was five times more than the lowest price. We had a deal killed one week before Completion Day with the official reason being attributed to cultural differences.

Hopefully you can see why I was motivated to write this book - so you have a chance to avoid a similar story happening to you!

What will the deal look like

Before you start dreaming about all the things you can do once you've sold your business, start considering the number of different types of deals that can be negotiated. The aim of negotiation is to create a deal that works for both parties (buyer and seller).

There are a number of different deal structures (known as the Consideration); here are the top four:

- Sell all your shares completely and walk away the day after the deal with the money, without having to remain in the business
- Agree to an earn-out, where you commit to staying with the company for an agreed time post sale and have agreed performance targets which pay-out when reached
- Sell your shareholding to the other shareholders in the business
- Complete a management buyout (MBO)

When selling your shares, you could receive one or more [illegible] cash, deferred cash (which is when cash is guaranteed to be given [illegible] date with no conditions attached), shares, deferred shares (which are [illegible] that have less rights than an ordinary share, i.e., no voting rights or dividend[illegible] only paid after a specific event has triggered, such as after all other classes of shares have been paid) or debentures (which is a type of loan without collateral).

You will also be asked to sign warranties, which is an assurance by one party to the other party that specific facts or conditions are true or will happen, and deeds (a legal document which confirms a transfer of an interest, right, or property) that commit to the best of your knowledge certain aspects of the business.

Indemnities may also be included. An indemnity is a sum payable from the seller (that's you) to the buyer, by way of compensation for a particular loss suffered by the buyer, discovered post completion.

Please don't let all these options and details scare you off. As and when the various choices and activities have to be decided, you'll have a team of experienced professionals to offer assistance and advice. The key right now is to just get a rough idea as to the various things that may happen.

What if I don't like the consideration

After initially instigating a sale, you might feel it's not in your best interest to proceed—perhaps you're not being offered fair market value, the price offered is too low, or the consideration doesn't feel right. You can always walk away. (In a future section, I cover how to work out your walkaway price.) Better yet, you can consider a backup plan.

essional managers to grow and run the senior management team, or going on a ıse your spirits and gain knowledge.

ny worth

analogy? A house's price is based on a location, how well it has been kept, its features, and how desirable it is in the eye of the beholder. It's an emotional sale; the prospective buyer should fall in love with your property, want it, and be able to visualise themselves living there. (Otherwise, if it's a buy-to-let investment—the investor needs to visualise as a good return on their investment.)

Valuing your business is very similar. It will depend on how well it is run, its business model, what else exists in the market, the potential buyer's own reason for buying it, and what it offers them in terms of a return on investment.

Valuing your company can be done using a number of financial models. The simplest way to get an idea of your value is to discover what similar businesses have sold for recently (similar size, industry, turnover, etc).

Failing that, another way to calculate a ball-park figure is to use an industry multiplier. Your business will have a market rate, which could be a multiple of your earnings before interest, tax, and amortisation (EBITA).

The multiple will be a higher number if you have reoccurring revenue instead of relying on future new orders, as it makes it easier to forecast and is more of a 'sure thing'. So, for example, if your turnover is £1.5 million, with a profit of £500,000, and the average multiplier in your industry is 5, you can apply a x5 multiple. Therefore, your business could be worth and sold for £2.5 million. If you forecasted your business for the next 3 years, hopefully profits will go up, thereby increasing the business' headline sale figure.

TIP: If a buyer offers you an EBITA multiple which is x8 or higher, logic says that it's most probably too much of a good thing. And if the multiple is x8 revenue definitely don't fall for it as it's a feint!

Another thought to consider is how many other businesses like yours are for sale. What market share do you have? With my business, we had the majority of market share. When compared to other businesses we were the only one left that could be easily purchased, as we owned the business without any external parties involved.

For more information on the different ways in which you can value your business using the different financial models visit http://www.SellYourBusiness.biz/store and purchase the 'Calculate Your Walkaway Price Pack'.

How can I achieve maximum value

There are a number of things you can do in order to achieve maximum value. One of which includes reading the rest of this book! I cover everything that is in your control, including; cleaning up all the areas of your business, making sure you work *on* the business and not *in* it, finding the right professional advisors, clearing out your skeletons in the business closet, how to ensure you hit your numbers, what a successful due diligence process is all about, and how to avoid a price chip. (A price chip is where the potential buyer revises their offer and reduces their offer price).

A word of warning, though: Value is in the eye of the beholder, so it's worth taking a look at what buyers look for in a business.

What do buyers look for in a business

Keep in mind you are selling your business for your own reasons. It's time to look at your business from a buyers' perspective, as they will be purchasing your business for their *own* reasons, which will differ from yours. They could be looking to purchase your company because:

- Your business is profitable.
- Your business offers them entry into a new market they have been eyeing for a while, and it will save them the time and money it would take to build.
- The prospective buyer could want to 'buy' your brand, reputation, people, products, services, and intellectual property, as it saves them from doing it all from scratch.
- Your business has clients they want to have on their books.
- Purchasing your business would increase their dominance in the market and increase market share.
- Buying your business will allow cost savings and consolidation, which will allow the combined business to be more efficient and profitable.
- It's a defensive reason and provides further protection from being acquired.

- It makes the combined entity more attractive for a future buyer.

What's also worth remembering is that there is also a broker's viewpoint. Just as estate agents love taking on 'easy to sell' properties, a broker will also look for an easy to sell business. Their criteria will be that it looks attractive, has a track record of being profitable, a good reputation in the market, solid numbers, a good forward order book, and a good story as to why now is the right time to sell. They don't like quirky businesses or owners who have changed their minds several times over the company's history.

Who's your buyer

Chances are you already know your future buyer even if you can't think of who it is today. The following are the three different types of potential buyers:

- Potential buyers who you know now (these are either individuals or organisations and include your suppliers, business partners, existing shareholders, employees (Management Buy Out), and competition)
- Potential buyers who you will know in the future
- Potential buyers who you will never encounter (this is because you don't know they are looking to acquire a business like yours, and they aren't yet aware your business exists and is on the market for sale.)

I suggest you start drawing up your list of potential buyers now and keep adding to it so that when you get to the future section, 'Finding a Buyer', you've already done some of the groundwork. You may have potential buyers in mind and have already been wooing them; make sure you add them to the list. Oh, and remember your competition can be added to the list as well. You can always have them join in the sale process later as they will already be familiar with the market and your business.

What should you personally expect during the sale process

It is very possible to run your business *and* prepare it for sale - businesses do this all the time, I did. But it's much better to prepare first, and then go to market. There's no doubt that it's going to be hard work, but considering your end goal, it should be worth it. In fact, you may find that you will start to look at your business in a different way, through 'new eyes', as you start to implement all the changes, recommendations, and tips in this book.

As a business owner who has invested your own money, time, and having poured your heart and soul into making the business work, expect an emotional roller coaster ride, because you've taken a baby business and nurtured it through its growth.

Every business owner I've spoken to thought they were prepared, yet were surprised about the toll it took on them—and this includes me! Remember, this has been your baby for a number of years, and you're in the process of letting it go, which is hard to do even if it's something you desire greatly. I don't have children, but perhaps it can be likened to a teenager finally flying the coop. On the one hand, you're excited to see them spread their wings, yet on the other hand, it's still sad to see them go!

After you've sold, it may take time for it to sink in, and there may be a hole that you will want to fill. When you look back at what happened, you might find that deciding to sell was an easy decision compared to every other decision that you subsequently make.

For me, preparing to sell was hard work and took longer than expected, but I survived. I'm sure you will too. I found that my emotions started to show while sale negotiations were in progress, and I encountered what is called 'deal fever'. Deal fever is when irrational thoughts start to happen, decisions are made because your emotions get caught up, and greed makes an appearance. You start to be carried away by the big numbers being talked about, and you start to believe that your company is worth more and that the potential buyer *definitely* wants to buy your business. In your head, you have already started to spend the money that you actually don't have.

Tip: Avoid deal fever! First of all, acknowledge that it exists. Realise that numbers will usually be reduced. Buyers will look for any reason to chip down the value, so it's best not to count your chickens until they've hatched.

Should you tell your staff

No, my suggestion is to avoid telling most of your staff at all costs. I cannot stress this strongly enough. You need to ensure that your staff not only continues to perform but actually, performs as best as they possibly can! If your staff discovers the business is for sale, they will experience the threat of change and the feeling of uncertainty. Whenever there's uncertainty, you'll be sure to find moral and productivity issues!

I'm sure you've experienced walking back into the office after something negative has happened within the organisation and felt the low energy and subdued staff? Selling a business—no matter what your reason—will never be perceived as positive news, so I urge you to withhold your intentions. Lastly, if employees knew the company was up for sale, what happens if it all falls through? That would create even more uncertainty and even larger morale and productivity issues.

What will happen to your employees post sale

There are various scenarios, and unfortunately, you cannot predict what the new owner will do. The worst case is that the new owner decides to let all your staff go in a shakeup. You can't stop this from happening; however, there are ways in which you can help your staff should this scenario arise, which I'll cover in later chapters. The best-case scenario is that by selling the business, you could be providing your staff with a new life—one with more security and more opportunity in terms of personal development and career progression. New buyers often inject a new energy and a variety of different perspectives that can enable employees to benefit.

I urge you not to worry about your employees. It's time to put yourself, your needs, and your family first. Your employees are paid to do their job, and you've looked after them. If you hadn’t, you wouldn't have a business today. Remember, your employees haven't taken the same risks you have over the years, and now is your time, not theirs. Furthermore, in many cases, a business sale often helps employees to better reposition themselves in or out of the organisation.

Selling your business is worth it

Why sell your business? Because it IS worth it, I promise. Remember the reason or reasons why you wanted to sell in the first place. Focus on the outcome and what you will get from the sale. If you are not sure, or you have forgotten, let me convince you by imaging the best scenarios for you. You have cash in the bank, and that gives you so many options. Just stop to think what you can have:

- Peace of mind as you've realised your business's return on investment
- Time to do all the things you wanted to do but were always too busy to do
- More time to spend with loved ones
- Funds to pay off your mortgage
- Funds to put your children through private school and pay for university
- Funds to get that fast car you've always wanted
- Funds that you can put towards a pension pot
- The option to start another business or become a business angel investor
- The option to become philanthropic and start giving back

It's very possible that the sales process may become quite a roller coaster ride. Many successful business sellers will attest to the highs and lows that the process brings. I suggest that you spend time drawing up a list or creating a picture of your ideal outcome. Write down what you want to do post sale, and make it as energising as possible.

When and if a day comes where you're questioning your strength, you'll have your list or picture to remind you what you're working toward.

I hope you're looking forward to your journey. It's exciting, and I assure you that it will be a worthwhile experience. Now that I have covered the reasons to sell your business, how to value your business, and a number of benefits that you could seize, it's time to move on to Part Two, and let me help you plan for your successful business sale by first preparing your business for sale.

Part Two – Is Your Business Prepared and Ready to Sell?

How close to ready is your business

Once you've made the decision to sell, the business needs to be ready *before* going out to the market, because once the ball starts rolling, juggling both the sale process and keeping the business going on a day-to-day basis is challenging. I ended up working 16 hour days for three months because I was preparing the business for sale while selling it. I highly recommend you don't follow my footsteps! Aside from avoiding long work hours, preparing prior to going to market will help you to:

- Free up time to maintain and grow the business
- Quickly navigate through the sales process by having the necessities prepared
- Find what you need, when you need it
- Keep the sales process quiet from employees
- Make the most of your staff's capabilities
- Pick the right kind of professional advisors for you
- Remove reasons the potential buyer can chip your valuation price down
- Complete the sales process the first time around

So before discussing corporate financers, accountants, and tax specialists, time is needed to get your house in order. Below I've listed all the things you can do starting now.

- Prepare the financials every way you can slice them

- Protect your business assets – legalities
- Get things in order and make plans to retain key staff – Human Resource (HR) planning
- Get operations humming
- Follow general housekeeping tips to give you an added edge
- Clear the skeletons out of the closet
- Work **on** the business, not **in** it

Along the way you may want to consider increasing profits, as that is a sure way to increase your business' valuation. We have a number of articles on **SellYourBusiness.biz** to help you achieve just that. The rest of this section will specifically focus on areas that need to be ready when preparing your business for sale.

Preparing the Financials Every Way You Can Slice Them

Make sure all your business's financial statutory information is up-to-date, including board minutes, and that dividend vouchers have been issued. Remember, your tax and VAT returns should be done on time, and all electronic paperwork records should be kept.

Have your annual accounts audited by a reputable accountancy firm—ideally, three consecutive years' worth, if your business has been going that long. It's good practice, provides buyers with comfort, and is a worthwhile independent check on your internal finance team performance. In some cases, an audit will be a necessary buyer requirement, so it's better to get it done now rather than having auditors rummage through your office, in addition to the buyer's due diligence team.

Annual accounts don't necessarily give an accurate picture of profitability and growth potential, so monthly Management Information (MI) is essential. It provides you, and the soon to be buyer, with the business heartbeat on how the business is doing.

If you don't have any management information reporting, now is the time to start and get ahead of the game. The potential buyer will want to get a feel for business trends and want to see monthly MI reports.

TIP: MI reports can be done retrospectively back to the beginning of your financial year, so you can track trends going forward. If you can create them for the last three years, that would be ideal to track the historic trends.

Management Information includes items that you want to measure and provide part of the picture as to how the business is doing. Example MI figures will include the targets, as well as actual figures, a comparison against the month before and year to date, as well as the current month's figures. Actual reported MI items should include the following:

- Headline profit & loss figures such as: total revenue for the month, cost of goods sold, operational costs, gross profit margin (=Gross Profit / Total Revenue)
- Order book value by product line

- Sales pipeline - how many are forecasted to close by when and how much
- Total number of clients
- Number of new clients
- Top 5 clients by revenue and % of overall business revenue
- Debtor days
- Stock control figures
- Number (and value) of transactions
- Number of employees
- Revenue per employee
- The figures for the 5 biggest cost areas in the business (salaries, property/office leases)
- Exceptional items expenditure
- Actual vs. forecasted/budgeted spend for specific budgets, e.g. marketing, IT, etc.

MI reports are best produced within a few days of months' end by your finance person, and provide a good indicator as to how things stand to meet future demand. You may discover what your return on investment is for marketing and how much each person is costing versus what they're bringing in.

You'll also want to analyse your costs (also known as cost lines) in finite detail. The reason behind this is so that the potential buyer can quickly find synergy and cost savings. Depending on what you are selling, this must be analysed by product line, per sale, or per service. For example, if you happen to sell hosted software services, work out what the infrastructure cost is and what the marginal cost of processing more (per transaction, operating a new service) is.

By analysing your cost lines you may find areas to cut or discover that you can re-negotiate your supplier contracts to get a better deal. Before you cut, make sure that that the value added will not be compromised by an inferior service.

Looking ahead, make sure that you have justifiable forecast information for the next three years, which has been built from the ground up, with full knowledge of your cost base. Your sales forecast should be in depth and linked to potential commission earnings. You must be comfortable with being able to achieve the numbers, because as the sale process progresses, the forecasts will be regularly reviewed against actual figures, and if they are lower than expected, it offers an opportunity for the potential buyer to revise their consideration offer downwards.

All this needs to be prepared before you find a buyer so that you can see where you can cut costs and provide this information quickly when asked for. That will make the due diligence easier, and employees and general business won't be disrupted.

If you need a Management Information Template, please visit the Sell Your Business Store where you'll find an Excel Template available for purchase: http://www.SellYourBusiness.biz/store

Sales and Marketing

Sales and marketing is where the meat of your revenue numbers comes from. Not only that, in a business sale process, your sales forecast is crucial and will help maximise your business valuation if you can quantify and qualify your sales pipeline, as it demonstrates the business potential which is going to be one of the reasons why the potential buyer is interested in you.

Make sure that you understand your sales orders pipeline forecast, qualify it and measure it. Place a realistic value on exactly when new orders will be given to your business. You will most definitely be asked for this information during the business sale process, and you may even have a dedicated meeting to go through the sales numbers and cost models so make sure that it stands up to scrutiny.

The Marketing function is very important as it supports the Sales function by generating leads, so broadcast the company brand internally and externally, communicate the business's mission, visions and unique selling points (USPs). Differentiate your business from the competitors and showcase your business's product and services.

Protecting Your Business Assets

Business assets range from owning property, patents, and intellectual property rights, including Internet domain names and trademarks, company vehicles, equipment, software licences, certification, non-disclosure agreements (NDA), and contracts. Make sure that you have all the proof paperwork at hand and all your contracts signed, as this ensures your business valuation holds, if not increases.

Whether you own or rent your property, make sure all the paperwork is up-to-date and in order. Make sure you know when your lease breaks are. This could be important during the sale process, as it will help buyer determine if they would want to exercise those breaks or not.

Carry out a software audit to determine how many licensed copies you have by comparing the number of software packages in use to the number of licence keys that your business owns. If the licence key information cannot be found, find the paid invoice associated with the software payment. If you cannot find evidence to back up your software license claim, you will have to budget to purchase software licences either outright in full or choose to lease software licences on a monthly basis.

TIP: If your business uses Microsoft software packages internally, make sure you have a Microsoft Action Pack (MAP) subscription, as you will save hundreds of pounds on dishing out software licence fee payments. MAP offers cost-effective savings for internal use of software licences such as MS Office and Windows operating systems.

Human Resource Planning – Getting Things in Order

Your staff will make a big difference in the success or failure of your business, and you need to make sure your business is legally covered with regards to its employees and contractors, especially as you plan to sell the business.

A potential buyer will expect that all your employees have a signed contract and adhere to a staff handbook. An employee handbook includes things like how employees can claim expenses, what the dress code is, how holidays are booked, and what the appraisal system is.

Ensure that each employee has read your policies and has agreed to comply with them in writing. In particular, employees must agree to their contract, staff handbook, health and safety policy, and IT and security policy.

If you have any contractors working for your business from time-to-time, make sure that they have signed contracts too.

Aside from all your policies being up-to-date, they need to be enforced. There is no point having an accident report book if it never gets filled out. Make a note of it, as this sort of information will be requested by your solicitor later in the sale process for the disclosure letter. (See Part Four for more details on what the disclosure letter includes.) If you haven't carried out an electrical socket test, this may be the time to do it.

Is your IT security policy current? What about your heath and safely policy, is it up-to-date? In our Free Documents Samples section on our Sell Your Business website we have a comprehensive checklist of policies available for you to use as a reference to help remind you what policies are right for your business, here: http://www.SellYourBusiness.biz/resources/free-document-samples/

How to Retain Key Staff

To minimise the risks during a sale, it is important to identify and encourage the retention of key employees. Some employee ideas include:

- Increase their notice period from one month to three months. (Anything more will raise alarm bells)
- Increase their base salary so that they are less likely to look elsewhere
- Increase their performance bonus earning structure, and make sure that it is achievable
- Increase their benefits (e.g., healthcare insurance to their family, dentist work coverage, etc.)
- Offer more holiday days, which is easier to introduce if they are long-service employees. This may incentivise others to stay longer

The earlier you do this while putting your house in order, the better.

If there is a key employee who is central to your business sale, you could take that person into your confidence and tell them about the sale. Additionally, offer a large financial bonus on successful business sale completion that will entice them to stay, as long as you feel they won't try and take further advantage of you and hold you to ransom during a crucial moment in the business sale process. It could be a bonus that will pay off their house mortgage. My recommendation is to associate the financial value with something, as its perception will be that it is worth more to that key employee.

It will be worth aligning your key employee interests with yours. The key employee will feel valued and trusted at being involved, can immediately see what's in it for them, and will work harder to help you achieve the goal, while you have an ally in the day-to-day business operations looking out for your interests more than ever.

Getting Operations Humming

An important part of operations, and an even bigger part of selling a business, is to ensure the business is protected in terms of its contracts with suppliers and customers. Make sure signed contracts exist for all of your suppliers and customers. The longer the term, the better for customers. If you have long-term contracts with your key suppliers, that will protect your cost base against future unexpected rising costs, and that's even better. Having unsigned client contracts will increase the risk of lowering your company valuation figure, so if you're getting started with making sure all your customer contracts are signed, start with your key customers (the ones that bring in the most revenue).

If you need a Contracts Summary Template, please visit the Sell Your Business Store where you'll find an Excel Template available for purchase: http://www.SellYourBusiness.biz/store

Ideally, you want 100% customer retention, even if its loss making, as having their name on your books may be worth it. Make sure that your customers are happy. Employ an account manager to manage your key customer accounts, and reward your account manager for customer retention and for growing accounts. Learn what your business excels at and what improvements can be made, and get them done.

If you have some key contracts that are due to expire during the sale process, try and get them extended now, offering a better price if needed, in order to protect your customer base, and by association, company valuation figure.

TIP: Have contracts available electronically, as the potential buyers will want to see them, and make sure that they are signed!

Operations must be aligned with the business vision, mission, and objectives. In this regard, processes must be documented and followed by staff members and management information should measure the results. This gives you the perfect opportunity to make sure that your processes are efficient and reflect the business as needed. Diagrams are always a big hit, as a picture is worth a thousand words, so use a drawing software package like Microsoft Visio or Omni Professional to help you or your staff.

If your business has a portfolio of products and services that are considered non-core because they're not aligned with the business vision, get rid of the non-core business now. Non-core business is going to distract the potential buyer, and may decrease the business valuation. If it's very profitable business, you can also set it up in a separate legal entity and have a contract between the businesses to carry out the services. This will aid quick disposal.

TIP: Do not commence any new ventures that require large capital expenditure or expand into a new market overseas

Make sure that the processes you have in place can be easily re-used without any rework for the business sale process. Without raising any questions, I had our key process documents updated on a regular basis as part of our normal business operations. During our internal meetings, the documents formed a cornerstone of discussion for everyone. An example of a key process document was our 'Product Development Roadmap.'

You must be able to understand what the effect is on your business should you lose one of your top 5 customers unexpectedly, or what the effect is on the sales pipeline if an expected win doesn't happen. In either case, make sure that you have a detailed plan in place which reduces the risk of losing that particular business, and even a back-up plan should the worst happen.

I learned about the effects of having unsigned contracts the hard way. During our business sale process, we lost a key customer's business. Luckily for us, the volume of new business achieved during the same period helped fill in some of the 'revenue hole', but it meant that our forecasts weren't as high as expected. Unfortunately, we lost 10% on our sales revenue forecast, causing a reduction in our overall valuation.

So avoid losing a large client by making sure that your contracts are signed. I made sure that it was in our sales peoples' best interests to have signed contracts by building it into the sales commission structure. Our sales people were rewarded more for signed contracts, and this helped prevent unsigned contracts for new business.

TIP: Reward your sales people for signed contracts by adding a 'contract signed' multiplier or bonus to encourage the salesperson to get the contract signed quickly. Consider having a sliding scale to

reward for quicker contract signing (higher in month 1, lower in month 2, lowest in month 3, no bonus if later).

There may be some situations in which a business will knowledgeably take on a financially loss-making contract. This may be because the initial contract will lead to bigger opportunities, or perhaps the business wanted to add the customer name to their list to associate more value to the business.

However, be careful, as you will be asked during due diligence exactly why you took on any loss-making business and what the clear plan is in order to make it profitable. If you can demonstrate the financial benefits to potential buyers, a price chip is unlikely.

In order to make sure that key documents, such as the sales pipeline forecast, customer contracts summary, and MI, are kept-up-to-date have individuals and teams responsible for them. Furthermore, reference all the key documents during internal meetings for past and future trends and statistics.

Another example is carrying out spot checks on documents that are referenced very infrequently, but are key during the sale process. For example, the fixed asset and software application asset registers will be needed, and this kind of information changes over time. Make sure that you or your finance person carries out random spot checks to ensure that the document is being kept up-to-date as part of everyday processes and procedures.

To make sure that all your business operations are running smoothly and efficiently, you should map all your current processes and tag them accordingly as runners, repeaters, and strangers in order to work out what can be improved upon. This is known as a lean technique for continuous improvement in the business. These can apply both internally as well as externally (for example, how you interact with your customers).

- Runners

  These are standard processes in your business that are carried out consistently and efficiently. Examples of runners would include the following:

  - The process used to recruit new staff members into the business, from making the decision to hire a new person, to engaging a recruitment agent with a brief, to carrying out the candidate interview process and sending out the offer or rejection letter

  - The sales process undertaken in order to close potential new business using the sales cycle process and procedures

  - The manufacturing process of a product, from the point of a sales order being raised, and it being produced in the factory, to leaving the warehouse to be shipped to the customer

- Repeaters

  These are less common processes and are usually less efficient than runners. Examples of repeaters would be processes that only happen once in a while, which may be a regular basis, such as carrying out an audit of your annual accounts. Another example would be a large order which requires some bespoke, manual work, and effort in order to fulfil the order.

- Strangers

> These are costly processes that should also be rare (because they are costly!). The cost is not only a financial one, but it's one of time, effort, and human resources. An example of a stranger may include a situation in which a brand new product is being brought to market, and everything is being done for the first time. As a result, the learning curve is steep, and the process is inefficient. Another example of a stranger is if the business goes for a huge tendering process, which requires all documentation and materials to be written for the first time. If a stranger process can be re-used while savings are made (thus more efficient), it will become a repeater.

The ideal situation is to have as many as runners as possible, with some repeaters, and only have one or two strangers (e.g., as a result of new business). This lean technique can also be applied to the manufacture of products.

Putting Your Best Foot Forward

Does your online presence (website, LinkedIn, Facebook, and Twitter pages) sell your company's products and services in the best possible light? If not, it's time for a makeover, and it's worth investing in writing new copy and giving it a new design. A side benefit to doing this is it helps with the sale documentation (read more in Part Four) and also when employees talk about their work, hopefully with pride. This ultimately helps increase productivity, friends and family can always have a quick look at the website and hopefully be impressed with what they see.

Having case studies written up and official sales marketing material available (all branded, of course) will help the prospective buyer with understanding the business and will present your business more professionally.

Before you enter the sale process, it's imperative to have your sales and marketing materials updated. Your website, brochures, and all other sales literature are an embodiment of the whole organisation. If they're outdated, disorganised, or broken, you'll have a variety of issues.

First, your corporate financier will have difficulties painting the best picture of your business. You don't want the financier using a 10 year old case study from your website, or create a marketing pack with an outdated version of your logo. Second, you're going to have to fix things on the fly as the financier works at making your proposition more attractive. And third, you're making it more difficult for the prospective buyer to envision going forward. The buyer ultimately wants to buy a great company that is great at telling the world how fantastic they are!

Stating that, now is not the time to necessarily rebrand yourself and engage in a long-term marketing overhaul, however, it's important to clean things up. Set aside a day or two to look at all your sales and marketing materials in an effort to create consistency, update outdated information, and make quick fixes.

In addition to your sales and marketing and on and offline messaging, make sure to include your social media accounts. Consistency is key. Make sure you have the same logo, same taglines, same profiles, same colours, correct addresses, and so forth.

TIP: Ask your marketing or admin person to print off every document that a client might see. This includes every web page, profile page, brochure, invoice, and so forth. You

can then lay everything out on the floor and immediately see if anything is inconsistent, old or no longer necessary.

General Housekeeping Tips to Give You an Added Edge

First impressions count, so spruce up the office, as during the sale process you will most likely be showing people around your work space. Make sure your offices are clean and tidy. Now is the time to get rid of clutter, if you have any. Apply a coat of paint, put up new pictures that demonstrate what your business is all about, add some plants, and get rid of that rickety desk. Make sure confidential company information isn't left lying around and posted on notice boards. Also get rid of any bad news, like the number of customer service complaints scribbled on whiteboards.

TIP: Introduce a clean desk policy and use the good reason 'to make it easier for the cleaners to do their job.'

If you've won any awards, show them off in the front desk reception area, and if you're a member of an association or sponsor charities, display your certificates and fundraising achievements. Don't forget about the toilet facilities either, as they leave an impression as well.

Make sure you have a central file server that has the right user and group access permissions set up and has a good structure. Get into the habit of scanning all documents (especially signed contracts) and keeping them on the file server. It will make it easier when all your signed sale contracts are suddenly requested. Backup your file server and test to make sure you can indeed restore from it if needed.

Web-based services such as Box.net or Dropbox.com are inexpensive file storage options, which are really handy to make sure there's an audit of who changed what file, and when. Even better, you have working backup and restore facilities available to you.

Clearing the Skeletons out of the Closet

No business is 100% squeaky clean. Mine wasn't. And that's only because you are busy getting on with the day-to-day running of the business and busy growing it.

Skeletons are anything that can adversely affect your sale process, whether they cause a delay or are used as a valid reason for a price chip.

When you find a skeleton, deal with it firmly and fairly. Don't leave any skeletons behind for discovery, and don't create any new ones. If you're going to keep some skeletons hanging, make sure that these are disclosed as early as possible in the sale process so that it can't be used as a reason for a price chip later.

Here are some skeletons that could be hanging in your closets right now:

- Someone in your business fired a past employee without just cause
- There are petty cash discrepancies, as a petty cash log file has not been kept
- Somebody has been using company resources for personal gain

- Failure to have enough software licenses to cover business operations
- Inappropriate accounting methods (tax evasion or avoidance)
- Illegal employees or employees with expired paperwork (e.g. Expired visa)
- Potential lawsuits

Either clean up your skeletons or be prepared to disclose them as soon as possible. Skeletons may become deal breakers or reasons for price chipping—both of which you want to avoid at all costs.

Getting You to Work on the Business Rather Than in It

If you're interested in selling up and shipping out the day after you complete the sale, it's extremely important to demonstrate that the business does not revolve around you. You may enjoy being the centre of attention and having your staff, customers, and suppliers rely on you for everything, but there's no way the buyer is going to let you ship out after handing over wads of cash. When selling your business, you do not want to be perceived as the most important person in making the business work.

This is where your employees and outsourced professionals come in. Learn the art of delegation, where you hand over responsibility to someone else. I know it's easier said than done, but it will be worth it. It's only a painful process if you let it be.

I liked delegating, as I enjoyed seeing my staff members grow in terms of personal development, plus it got rid of the stuff that I didn't want to do (the benefit of being a boss)! I kept a longer-term view in mind, which would lead to me being able to exit the business quickly, without negatively affecting the valuation. At least that was the plan. What really happened was our sale process took so long, and I became exhausted from it all. I actually left the business as an employee, demonstrating that the day-to-day business did run smoothly, leaving my business partner to make the strategic decisions as needed.

I was lucky to have recruited great people, and the culture was one of taking responsibility. Instead of employees asking for permission, I promoted the idea of asking for forgiveness, if ever needed, after making decisions themselves.

And yes, you have to let your staff make mistakes, willingly; it's one way of learning, from their own mistakes. Even though it's a natural reaction, don't jump down their necks when they make a mistake. Support them, ask them what they would have done differently in hindsight, and watch them grow in confidence.

If they continue to make the same mistake over and over again, that's the time to step in and work out what's happening and why the same decision is being made. What factors are they basing their decision on? Is it really a mistake? What's the negative outcome that's causing it to be treated as a mistake? Also, realise there's more than one way to skin a cat. A solution may not be your solution, but it's a solution just the same. Keep reminding yourself, that the company needs to operate without you.

My office door was always open. Everyone could just pop in to talk over a situation, and I would refuse to give them the answer on a silver platter. They had to come with their own options as to what the solution or answer was. Most of the time, I didn't have to do anything except nod and agree, and other times, I helped guide them to the right decision by making them think for themselves.

TIP: Make it a policy that whenever an employee comes to you with a problem that they must also come with a couple possible of solutions in mind. This will force them to start thinking about solutions rather than relying on you for the answers.

If you have a large enough business, build and empower your management team to look after the day-to-day business. If you're a smaller business, look to promote a second-in-command, or hire someone in to take the daily business pressure off you.

If you are wondering how you know you're working on the business and not in it, consider the following:

- You should be spending the majority of your time looking at the business' future and how to maximise it. This could be:
  - Having lunches with people that are supporting sale process needs
  - Having conversations with potential joint-venture partners that will inject more value into the company
  - Studying ways to increase profits and reduce costs
  - Spending more time literally out of the business premises
- You should be satisfied with understanding how the business is doing through its Management Information reports alone

- You should be able to make strategic decisions quickly or react to something quickly if needed, without increasing the number of hours you work
- You should be making sure that all invoicing happens on time
- If you have employed account manager(s), you should not be speaking to your customers on day-to-day account business
- You should *not* be worrying about unpacking the latest stationary order that just arrived at the office

If you want to walk away from the business with no strings attached, the attitude that 'If you want something done right, you have to do it yourself', must go!

Now that you have time to put your feet up, relax, and think things through (because you're working on the business and not in it), let's reflect on what else I have covered in this section. No corner should have been left unturned in your business. I hope you've already found ways to squeeze some more costs out of your business, as well as getting all those hard worked for contracts signed. Putting your ear to the ground should find that your operations are humming nicely. Your staff should be motivated and busy being productive. Everyone should understand the objectives which are reflected in your management information reports. And you should be receiving the MI reports on time and using them to judge how the business is doing.

As you've spent a fair amount of time and effort preparing your business for sale, it's time to put it to the test! In the next section I will be covering how to choose your business sale team members with care. Who they are, what role they will be playing as part of your team, and what deliverables are to be expected from each of the team members in order to achieve a successful sale for your business will be covered.

Part Three – Do You Have Your Dream Business Sale Team in Place?

Now that you've prepared your business for sale and are spending more time on the business than in it, it's time to get your business sale team in place before going out to the market to find a buyer.

Selling is a team effort, and I recommend surrounding yourself with the best team possible. The team should consist of trusted employees from the business and external professional advisors who will only be involved with the actual sale process.

Here's a snapshot of what I'm going to cover in this section that will help you get ready for sale:

- Consider what members you need for your success team
- Engage a business broker
- Instruct your corporate solicitor
- Use an accountant
- Know what a tax advisor is needed for
- Plan with a financial advisor
- Beauty parade your professional advisors
- Find out who's personally rooting for you
- Assess whether or not all preparations are completed

Who You Will Need Internally as Part of Your Success Team

Ideally, as I covered in the previous chapter, you should be free from running the business on a day-to-day basis, so having a senior management team, or at least an operations lieutenant, to deal with the day-to-day will achieve three very important objectives.

Firstly, it will release you to focus on the sale process. Secondly, it will free your time to ensure that the business continues to hit its numbers against forecasts, while overseeing the senior management team. Thirdly, when you sell, you will be more likely to walk away, rather than be tied into an earn-out clause. Luckily, I started building up my senior management team a year before my business partner and I agreed to sell.

Make sure that you have a person who will deal with the numbers; this could be your financial controller, finance director, or even yourself. This person needs to know a business sale is on-going, and be prepared to slice and dice the numbers in all sorts of ways (as detailed in Part Two) at the request of your potential buyers. Aside from having the numbers at hand, this person needs to be capable of explaining them as well.

If you develop products, your team needs someone who understands how the products are developed and its architecture; normally, this is your development manager or equivalent. Conversely, if you're in professional services, you will need someone who understands the processes from start to finish; usually your quality assurance compliance officer is a good place to start. If it's manufacturing, your operations manager running the factory or warehouse will be key.

During the sale process, you will need to keep a very close eye on cost expenditure control, even if you have delegated this to your financial controller or finance director. If the business purchases or commits to a high value supplier contract, the buyer may knock the price down, as it requires them to honour the commitment when it may reduce their return on investment. In order to effectively manage this, make sure that any expenditure over a certain amount must be approved at board or senior management team level.

As previously mentioned in Part One, the fewer number of people in the know, the better. You want the business focused on the day-to-day business operations. However, the news could leak out. Employees could guess that a sale is in progress due to all the necessary preparation. Strangers visiting the premise could cause rumours. Demands for data and reports which must be turned around within a short period could result in questions. Employees could bump into someone at a trade sale who mentions that they've heard on the grapevine that your business is up for sale. I can't stress enough how important it is to prepare the business first, and then go to the market! That's why I'm here to help you achieve just that, which will reduce the risk of the news leaking out from your business itself.

TIP: Time spent on preparing your business for sale is worthwhile, as it will reduce the risk of exposure

In my business, only three people knew we were up for sale—our part-time financial controller, myself, and my business partner—and we had over 40 staff in the business at the time. Later on in the process, after I left the business as an employee, two members of the senior management team (the development manager and the operations director) became aware of the sale process.

From an internal perspective, you need to consider all the things that must be done. You'll then want to decide what you're best at doing, and delegate the rest. When delegating, those that know the business is being prepared for sale will require little explanation when receiving new tasks. For those unaware of the sale, you can simply announce that you're on a drive to make the organisation more effective and efficient.

If you have one or more business partners in the business you could delegate the tasks out between you. One partner could focus on the business sale, the other on driving the business and making sure that the business continued to perform which demonstrated increase in revenues and clients, which in turn will help maximise the business valuation.

Engaging a Business Broker

The most important external advisor is your business broker (also known as a corporate financier), who will manage the entire sale process for you. The broker may be an individual person, a boutique mergers, and acquisitions (M&A) company, or anything in between.

These guys and gals look great in suits. They are good at marketing, have the killer instinct, know their numbers, can sell and negotiate, don't get emotionally involved as they view it as a 'transaction', and will run the process for you to the best timeline possible. They are there to maximise your business's valuation. They will make sure that they get as many potential buyers to the table at the same time, run the bidding process, maintain the best price through the negotiations, and close the deal for you.

You want to choose a broker that has the right connections, a good success track record, and ideally experience in your industry. Here's a checklist of what they will do:

- Provide guidance throughout the whole process, which includes advising you on any pre-sale issues that should be taken care of, and provide information on how they see your business valuation, given the market and deals recently completed
- Help you draw up the list of potential buyers
- Prepare and distribute the marketing material in order to promote your business to interested parties
- Qualify all interested party responses by communicating with them and finding out if they have the means to pay-out
- Help you through the due diligence process
- Advise you on offers received and lead on negotiations with all potential buyers
- Help your solicitor complete the deal

Corporate financial advisor fees may seem rather expensive when taken on their own, but in the bigger context of the sale, they are there to help you close the deal. It's important to know fees can be negotiated, and their charges can be based on success. Examples of broker payment structures include:

- £30k upfront fee with 3% of the total consideration on completion

- £25k upfront free with 3% of the first £2m total consideration on completion and then 1% on the rest
- No upfront fee with 4% of the total consideration on completion
- A negotiated fixed fee of £100k for selling a company worth £4m

TIP: You can work out a two-tier fee structure for corporate financiers; have a more expensive price for successful completion and a cheaper one if not.

The broker will draw up the terms of engagement which normally take the form of a 2-4 page letter. It will include the fee structure, what they will and won't do as part of the process, and cancelation terms.

Depending on your business circumstances, you could engage a broker to sell your business to a single target, a pre-defined number of targets, or the whole market. In my experience, you should go out to the whole market to increase your chances of being successfully sold for the price you want. This is, of course, unless you already started discussions with a single party and just want to complete the deal with them.

Before you agree and sign the terms of engagement with a broker, be careful of 'long tail' termination clauses. These are used by corporate financiers who will still collect their fee if you sell to a buyer they introduced you within a year (or more depending on the terms you signed) of when they stopped working for you, before either party terminated the engagement.

TIP: Negotiate long tail termination clauses with your corporate financer carefully, as a situation where you change corporate financiers may arise.

During our many sale attempts over the years, we used five different brokers from different companies and sizes. I learned that you don't have to like your advisor, but it helps if you respect them. You want to be able to listen and take their professional advice, especially during times when deal fever takes over. That's why it's so important to beauty parade and take your time when choosing a broker.

As the expression goes, 'you have to earn respect', so make sure you get to know the broker as a person, as well as a professional. Also, use their credentials and appreciate their keenness to complete the transaction. With one brokerage firm we bought into a particular broker, only to be allocated a different inexperienced person to sell the business once we engaged them. Make sure that you meet the actual broker you will be working hand-in-hand with before agreeing to retain an organisations' services.

With another organisation, we found that they treated the sale process as an auction and rushed to tell everyone and anyone about our offer. It felt as if they were rushing us and the process through a sausage machine. This may be the 'right way' for some businesses, but it wasn't for ours.

On http://www.SellYourBusiness.biz/store, we have a comprehensive 'The Seller's Professional Advisors Beauty Parade Pack' available to make sure you have plenty of questions to ask each professional advisor, and a scoring sheet to make it easier for you to review your candidates before making your final decision.

Instructing Your Corporate Solicitor

You may already have a solicitor the business has used for legal purposes, however, you will need a corporate solicitor who's a business sale specialist, as they will be aware of the tricks within the legal contracts and advise you accordingly.

You will be spending a lot of time with your corporate solicitor once you've found potential buyers. Make sure they have a bit of depth in their team, to be able to react quickly and push the sale through on a tight timescale. They will be focused on making sure all the legal documentation, including the Sale Purchase Agreement (SPA) document, is ready for signature on Completion Day, and also looking after the funds.

TIP: Find out from your corporate solicitor which brokers they have worked with before, as it may be advantageous to work with the same team members.

Solicitor's fees can be expensive; however, realise that you can negotiate different fee types and in some cases agree to a combination. Examples include:

- Fixed fees – A fixed figure that is paid when the deal is successful, regardless of how long the sale process takes

- Capped fees – Fees are capped at a pre-agreed financial number
- Contingent fees – These are fees, which you pay at a reduced cost if the deal doesn't complete

Using an Accountant

If you don't have a financial controller or finance director, I strongly recommend you elicit the help from your accountancy firm, as they will already be familiar with your business. If you don't have an accountant, hire one to assist you instead of trying to do all the numbers yourself. The accountant will provide all the financial documentation including business tax and VAT information, and be able to answer all the financial due diligence questions that arise. Your accountant will likely work closely with your chosen business broker in order to provide the financial material needed (for example, the profit & loss, balance sheet, as well as the three year forecast, or business cost models).

You could hire the accountant as an employee, full or part-time, or as a consultant on a daily rate.

What a Tax Advisor is Needed For

Your tax advisor will make sure that the deal is tax efficient, apply for tax clearance on your behalf, and assist you on personal tax planning post completion.

Tax clearance is when your tax advisor writes to HM Revenue & Customs (HMRC) on your behalf, informing them of the deal structure. The advisor will then get a reply, in the form of a tax clearance letter, back from HMRC after they have reviewed the details. The HMRC will confirm whether or not they are happy with the deal structure and will not challenge it once the deal has completed. This will give you certainty on the tax liability that will be owed to HMRC as well as also confirming whether or not you are eligible for Entrepreneur's Relief. Tax clearance can take anywhere from a couple weeks to a month.

TIP: If you choose not to use a tax advisor, your solicitor should be able to obtain tax clearance for you.

Your tax advisor will be valuable to you when you have a number of consideration offers on the table that look wildly different and have huge implications on tax calculations. The biggest number deal might not be the best for you, as it may leave a deeper hole in your pocket in cash terms— for example, if you are given the following two offers to choose from:

- Offer A: £200,000 cash on completion
- Offer B: £100,000 cash and £400,000 worth of shares in the purchaser's company on completion

Assume you are eligible for entrepreneur's tax relief at 10%. You will need to pay the taxman the full amount due as per HMC&E rules:

- Offer A tax to pay: £20,000, leaving you with £180,000 cash in your pocket
- Offer B tax to pay: £50,000, leaving you with £50,000 cash in your pocket

Offer B looks better on paper, but Offer A gives you more cash in your pocket. The shares may be worth more or less, and you could have restrictions on when you can sell them. Therefore, you may choose to take Offer A as it is more of a 'sure' thing.

Note: To keep this example simple, it excludes the costs of selling.

Financial Planning with a Financial Advisor

You may think it's counting your chickens before they hatch, but you should find a financial advisor *before* the deal is completed. It will take time to find the right financial advisor that you feel comfortable with, and although you might think its financially prudent to have a lot of cash sitting in a low-interest account, it could be riskier if it's with just one bank as you will (hopefully) be over the savings safety net, otherwise known as the Financial Services Compensation Scheme (FSCS) limit!

Investing your share of the sale could also have tax implications, which is better to know before the sale completes. Please seek professional advice, but just as an example, your financial advisor could advise you that you should become a non-resident in the UK to be most tax efficient!

Beauty Parading Your Professional Advisors

As shown above, selling requires professional advisors, such as a business broker, solicitor, tax advisor, financial advisor, and accountant. Getting the right professional advisors on board is worth every penny, and it will add value to your business sale. But you have to choose wisely. It is worth taking your time to choose, as you could be working with them for some time. Make sure you interview at least three professional advisors for each role.

Obtain referrals from other business owners who have sold, and find out what made those business owners pick those advisors. Once you have some names, find out their recent track record. Get them to pitch to you and tell you why you should give them your business. Go meet them in their offices, see how they treat you, what team they bring in for the pitch, and ask them lots of questions. I asked a few when we beauty paraded potential corporate solicitors, and in hindsight, I should have asked more! Some of those questions are the following:

- What were the last 10 deals they successfully completed?
- Who facilitated those deals?
- Have they completed deals in your market?
- Have they already sold to a potential buyer you have in mind?
- How do they keep tension if there's only one interested buyer party?
- Are those pitching to you going to be the ones working on your deal?
- How are the ones working on your deal incentivised?
- Did they list some potential buyers?
- Did they outline the sale process steps?

- Do they have enough manpower?
- How many other deals are they working on at the same time, and what stage are those deals at?

During the pitch, also note if you feel a connection with the people that presented. You will need to be able to trust your advisors, and be prepared for unexpected events, such as an advisor taking some holiday at a crucial time (regardless if their phone would be on all the time) or deciding to change firms during your sale process, which happened to me.

TIP: When you interview your potential broker, ask them what challenges they see when looking at your business to sell.

On **SellYourBusiness.biz**, to help you interview your professional advisors, don't forget that we have a complete list of questions with a scoring card that will make it easier for you to interview your professional advisors against a benchmark in the 'The Seller's Professional Advisors Beauty Parade Pack'.

Who's personally rooting for you?

Find an independent advisor, a confidant if you will, to pour your heart out to, who's not part of the process and doesn't have a vested interest in your business. You want someone that will look out for your best interests and can give clear-headed, sound advice, especially in times of 'deal fever'. Ideally, that confidant will be another business owner who has 'been there and done it' themselves—like me!

Agree to certain rules with your confidant. For example, if your confidant spots your stress levels increasing to a dangerous point and tells you to go take a day off, do it. Sometimes you cannot see beyond your own line of vision, and you will need a little help with perspective. Listen to what they are telling you. It's non-negotiable, and you will feel better for it as a small break every now and then will give you a few moments to clear your head, re-energise and start fresh the next day.

Aside from your independent advisory, and if you happen to have a business partner, take turns driving the process forward, and take over for each other to help reduce stress levels and keep energy levels up. Delegate when you can, and always ask for help when you need it. This is a team process, and though you can do it all by yourself if you want to, the easier route is to make the most of the team around you and letting them help and support you.

Also consider having a couple friends on speed dial who don't know the sale process is going on. It's good to just have dinner with them from time to time and forget about the sale process for a couple of hours—especially useful if you're in a tough point in the process. Go out to a movie with your partner. Enjoy the perks of happy-hour after work with some friends. Just take a little bit of time for yourself to clear your head and rejuvenate.

Regarding family, my recommendation is to keep your family in the dark, and this includes your home partner. But this is a personal choice and *entirely* up to you. You know best. Just be aware that it's going to be quite a roller coaster ride, and if they are riding that emotional journey with you, it's going to heighten everything. This will be difficult. Your partner, who could be your best friend, may or may not understand the late hours and need to work late. Your children may wonder why you aren't home for dinner some nights. Stay strong. You will need their support, and if they are going with you through the emotional ups and downs of the sale process with you, it may make it difficult for them to be the strong shoulder to rest on.

Look after yourself both physically and mentally. Take breaks frequently. Set up a routine, and keep to it. Exercise regularly. This will not only help to keep you physically fit, but it will also help to get your adrenaline going and kick start your endorphins, leaving you mentally and emotionally well. Eat healthy foods, as this will keep your insulin levels steady. Get enough sleep, and make sure that you remain hydrated (with water!). All these things will help you stay strong throughout the process. You're going to need to keep your energy levels up, especially when it starts getting tough, which we all know is harder to do in stressful periods.

TIP: I found a couple of hours a week on either a squash or tennis court was a great stress reliever and helped me re-energise.

Are all preparations completed?

Hopefully, Parts Two and Three of this book have helped you prepare your business for sale, and assisted with your search for external professional advisors. You are now ready to go to market with the comfort of an efficiently run business, and a business sale team ready to go to work to realise your maximisation valuation.

Right, ready? Raring to get started on finding a buyer? Great. Be prepared for a marathon, not a sprint.

Go on a holiday before you start looking for a buyer. This achieves two things. It should prove the business can run without you, and you're rested up and ready to start.

Let us begin.

Part Four – Are You Ready to Seal the Deal on the Market?

By now, you have hopefully learned how to look after the HR side of things, improve your business processes so that management information can easily be reported on, and have streamlined your operations, thus creating efficiencies which will protect future revenues and reduced costs.

You should also have your success team in place and have engaged your external professional advisors. By spending time preparing your business and having met with your team, you likely have a more meaningful understanding of what your business is worth, how valuable you are to the business, and what considerations will most likely be offered. For example, if your presence in the business is no longer needed, your consideration may not include an earn-out for yourself.

The Business Sale Steps

1. Create a list of buyers
2. Create the teaser letter and prepare for issuing
3. A potential buyer expresses interest
4. Get a Non-Disclosure Agreement (NDA) signed by any interested party
5. Send the Memorandum of Information (MOI) to any interested parties
6. Potential buyer proceeds or drops out
7. Meet the potential buyer face-to-face and give a presentation
8. Indicative offers received
9. Shortlist potential buyers

10. Due diligence is performed
11. Final offer letters are issued
12. Completion

The business sale process is a fluid one. It's akin to an athletic track race in which athletes start at different points along the track, and ideally, they all cross the finish line very close to each other. Expect buyers to join from the start of the process and others to join after it's started and even later on. This is a management task for your broker, and so he will speed up or slow down the process to accommodate potential buyers, in order to maximise competition to keep the valuation high.

Creating a List of Buyers

Creating your list of potential buyers is like creating your sales pipeline. The reason sales pipelines are as fat as possible at the top of the funnel is because the conversion rate reduces the numbers in the end that will purchase from you. This is where having the right broker makes a huge difference, as they will have connections, and as part of their offered services, your broker will come up with a list of potential buyers.

It's always easier to eliminate than add to the list, so make sure that the list is as long as possible. First, brainstorm 100 potential buyers:

- Include companies that have recently acquired in your market or are adjacent to it
- Include your competition. (You can always add them into the process at a later stage, after newcomers)

- Include companies from overseas that don't have a presence yet in your geographic market
- If appropriate, include your biggest customers
- Include private equity firms. These are firms which invest on behalf of endowments, foundations, pension funds, and other institutions
- Include venture capital funds. Venture capitalists will invest alongside management in companies and will expect an exit in the future in order to have a return on their investment
- Carry out research and look for companies using Internet search engines

Once the list is compiled, the next step is to qualify the companies on the list and shortlist them by answering the following questions:

- Can the buyer afford to buy your business?
- How much spare cash does the buyer have?
- Are they currently on an acquisition trail?
- Is your business a natural strategic fit?
- Do you know who to target and are they the right person to get 'in'?

Once you and your business advisor have shortened the list, you can then agree on who will be approached, and when. You could go for the rifle shot approach of choosing two or three to begin with or start with twenty.

Creating the Teaser Letter

The purpose of the teaser letter is to make the market aware that your business is ready to be acquired, should the right opportunity arise, and to identify potential interested buyers.

It is generally a two page document, which is written by your broker (as one of their agreed deliverables for their fee) with your input, to showcase your business to potential interested parties who may or may not be actively acquiring businesses at this precise moment in time. The letter will most likely contain the following:

- The broad type of business it is
- Your headline financial figures (profit, revenue)
- Reason for sale
- Outline the opportunity without mentioning names
- Your broker's contact details to request more information

The teaser letter should avoid stating an asking price or even a range. You don't want to put someone off before it's even begun. If you would like to see a teaser letter in all its glory, we have an example on our website here:

http://www.SellYourBusiness.biz/resources/free-document-samples

Depending on the potential buyer's organisational structure, your broker may make a call before sending out the letter. The letter is normally sent directly to the managing director/chief executive, to the financial director, or to the acquisitions manager/director.

What to Do When a Potential Buyer Expresses Interest

After receiving the teaser letter, your broker will follow up with a call to find out if the potential party is curious and interested and what attracted them to your business. This allows your broker to discuss the opportunity in more detail and qualify the interest of the potential buyer some more. If your broker is not familiar with the interested party, they will check up on the company's financials and work out if they have the means to pay-out, as well as see if there is strategic value in the potential acquisition. If the party is still interested, the broker will send the potential buyer a confidentiality agreement (a.k.a. a non-disclosure agreement) to sign before releasing further details.

Signing the Non-Disclosure Agreement

The non-disclosure agreement (NDA) is a standard business sale NDA and is drawn up by your broker. It covers the discretion for both parties, to make sure that both parties keep all matters confidential and only provide information to other parties (such as solicitors) on a need-to-know basis, and should any paperwork or documentation be exchanged, the return of them should either party withdraw their interest.

Once the NDA is signed, the broker discusses the opportunity with the interested party in more detail and sends the Memorandum of Information (covered more in-depth below) to the interested party.

Enforcing a signed NDA is difficult should any of its terms be breached, as the injured party must prove the source of the leak and legal costs are expensive. However, at the signing of the NDA, it should be mentioned that you take the importance of confidentiality very seriously, and that if breached, you will be seeking legal counsel. Then, end on a positive note by saying that you are certain they will uphold their end of the confidentiality bargain and that you will also honour any information that they deem as private as well. For an example of what a non-disclosure agreement business sale document looks like, visit:

http://www.SellYourBusiness.biz/resources/free-document-samples

Sending the Memorandum of Information

The Memorandum of Information (MOI) is a selling document that should be no more than 20 pages. It showcases your business in detail and will be written by your corporate financial advisor (as part of their engagement and fee), after they have spent hours interviewing you and anyone else in your business who is 'in' on the sale, and before going out to market. This document needs to be reviewed by your success team members for accuracy, and include the following sections at a minimum:

- Executive summary
- Brief history of business
- Organisational structure, employee numbers, and biographies of key individuals
- Shareholding structure
- Customers and markets
- Sales and marketing
- Products and Services descriptions
- Future developments and opportunities
- Facilities
- Financial information, such as three years' historical accounts, revenue split by product/service, forecast for next 3 years (sales, gross profit and EBITA), as well as sales forecast projection.

For an example of what the table of contents is for an Memorandum of Information, visit:

http://www.SellYourBusiness.biz/resources/free-document-samples

The MOI is most likely to be sent in a nice bound document via courier post, in order to restrict the numbers in circulation.

What to Do When Potential Buyers Are Still Interested or Drop Out

Once the potential buyer has received the MOI, the broker will keep in regular contact to check if they are still interested, generally this is by phone or email. If they are not interested, the broker should find out why (perhaps something in the MOI put them off when it shouldn't have) and see if they can keep them interested. Otherwise, the potential buyer needs to return to your broker or confirm they destroyed the MOI. If still interested, the next step is a face-to-face meeting between the two parties (the potential buyer and the seller).

Before meeting with potential buyers for the first time, your broker will have put together a management presentation that extracts the essentials from the MOI document, and also demonstrates the opportunity. The presentation should be no more than 10-15 slides and last half an hour. For more information on what should be included in the slides, visit http://www.SellYourBusiness.biz/resources/free-document-samples

Make sure that the management presentation flows well, and practice dry run-throughs several times in front of your broker, who will take on the role as the potential buyer, until it is smooth as silk. If more than one person is presenting, agree who will present which slides to the potential buyer. For example, I presented the figures and products and solutions, while my business partner set the scene and outlined what the future opportunities were. We also made sure we marked our slides so we knew where our handover points were.

Find out exactly whom it is you are meeting with, and strategise why the potential buyer is interested so that the meeting can be tailored accordingly. Don't draw any conclusions before the meeting, as the wrong track could be taken. Just make some assumptions and look to confirm if the assumptions made are correct or not during the meeting.

Think of the meeting as a first date, it's wooing time. Both sides of the date are going to be dressed to impress, on their best behaviour, and showing their best side.

The meeting should be held in a formal setting, offsite (not at your business premises), and as a general rule of thumb, your broker hosts the meeting in their offices. Expect and make sure that the first meeting doesn't last more than two hours. This gives plenty of time for questions to be asked from both sides of the table and for rapport to build between the two parties at the table. The meeting should not be held over a meal, nor should you go out drinking with them!

At the end of the meeting, your broker will outline what the next steps are and state the deadline for receiving indicative offers from potential buyers.

You may be asked to meet one or two times more as the potential buyer may want to send in different people to attend. Always meet on neutral territory, ideally at your broker's offices. Potential buyers will have the chance to visit your business' premises later in the process.

Receiving Indicative Offers

Your broker will be busy encouraging potential buyers to express their continued interest and intent to purchase by asking for their indicative offer and trying to increase the indicative offers as much as possible.

Indicative offers may be initially offered over the phone when the potential buyer is talking to your broker, as it is a way of tentatively figuring out what the lay of the land is and what price range is acceptable.

Formal indicative offers will be made by letter on the potential buyer's letterhead paper, referred to sometimes as heads of terms agreement. It will include details of their offer, which is normally made on a 'cash and debt-free' basis, and will contain particulars on the consideration.

A 'cash and debt-free' basis means that the purchase price offered will be adjusted up or down, depending on the company's financial position at a given time, to reach the actual purchase price. Any cash or cash equivalents owned by the company will increase the purchase price, while any debt will decrease the purchase price.

How the final purchase price is determined is an integral part of the share purchase agreement, and it is often intensively negotiated between the buyer and the seller. There are two different approaches: the closing balance sheet adjustment and the fixed purchase price or a locked box mechanism. While the closing balance-sheet adjustment is easier to calculate, you may find that the locked box mechanism is better for you and your business, I'll cover the locked box mechanism in more in detail in Part Five.

The consideration is a fancy term for the terms of the deal. Its actual definition is 'anything of value promised to another when making a contract'. The consideration is not only cash, but could include shares, debentures, warranties, deeds, as well as an earn-out. I cover the consideration in more detail below at the best and final offer stage.

Suffice to say at this point, the indicative offer will contain a headline figure and be very light on detail. It may include the potential buyer's desire to keep the shareholders on or not.

If you don't like the offer (because the figure is too low or the consideration make-up is too much paper and not enough cash), don't worry. This is just the starting point for negotiations, and just like house prices, the value can go up and down over the course of the sale process. The indicative offer at this stage separates the interested parties from potential buyers who should have the means to pay and intend to do the deal.

Short-listing Potential Buyers

When deciding which potential buyers should be short-listed, they must have all submitted an indicative offer, which is then used as part of the criteria for short listing. A number of things should be looked at including:

- What is the consideration made up of?
- Does the potential buyer have the means to pay?
- Is the potential buyer actually on a fishing expedition?
- Is there an earn-out for specific individuals?

- Are there any specific exclusions or additions in the offer?
- How much cash is being offered on completion?
- Will you have enough cash to pay the taxman?
- What is likely to happen to the business post sale?

Determining which consideration offer is better than the other also requires a lot of thought.

Remember, I'm looking to maximise the amount of money (i.e., cash) you have in your pocket at the earliest opportunity. This is best shown in the example that follows, which looks at different instruments that can be used in order to pay the consideration. I look at it from the position of how much cash I have in my pocket *after* all costs and charges have been deducted that relate directly with the sale, as cash equals certainty. This includes paying the taxman, and I'll show you why it's so important to factor in the taxman.

When you sell a business in the UK, as it is a business asset, capital gains tax will apply, which at the time of this writing is 28%. However, if you are entitled to Entrepreneur's Relief, it will reduce your CGT to 10%. ER is a lifetime allowance and applies to the first £10milion.

To reduce your tax bill, if you are a non-UK resident, before selling your business you may qualify, however you need to seek professional advice before making any decisions, as the rules may change.

I've listed each available instrument in order of their 'most wanted' factor:

- Cash on completion is the best thing to have
- Deferred cash is the next best thing to have

- Debentures, drawn on a bank account, could be worth it, as it's a loan note you can cash in at an agreed future date. However, there is a small risk that the bank goes bust
- Shares on completion may be worth having (it's paper-based, so it has a greater level of uncertainty when compared to cash)
- Shares at a future date may be worth having
- Cash offered as part of an earn-out may be worth having
- Shares offered as part of an earn-out may be worth having

With both cash and shares that are part of an earn-out, you have the *opportunity* of making more money – this is not a guarantee by any means, and only pays out if certain milestones are achieved. As we all know, the value of shares can go up or down over time.

- Buyer 'A': £1.5m cash on completion
- Buyer 'B': £1m cash on completion, plus earn out of £5m over two years
- Buyer 'C': £1.5m cash plus £0.5m shares on completion, plus earn out of £3million over 3 years
- Buyer 'D': £1.5m cash on completion, plus £0.5m deferred cash two years later
- Buyer A: Total potential value £1.5m of which all of it is guaranteed
- Buyer B: Total potential value £6m of which £1m is guaranteed
- Buyer C: Total potential value £5m of which £1.5m is guaranteed
- Buyer D: Total potential value £2m of which all of it is guaranteed

I highly recommend involving your tax advisor at this point, as they will indicate which consideration is best in terms of how much tax you will pay out, and *when* you need to pay it. The example here is if the deal is closed with Buyer D, tax on £2m will need to be paid.

Don't get carried away by the consideration at this point, because it's not the only factor to take into consideration!! (Excuse the pun!) You also need to think about what the company's future is post sale, especially if the offer includes an earn-out for you to achieve.

Tip: Before you make any short-listing decisions, draw up a pro/con list of each indicative offer and sleep on it.

If you only have one indicative offer, the broker should be working on bringing more potential buyers on board in order to create competition and can slow the process down accordingly in order to have parties at the same point in the process. If the decision is to continue, I strongly recommend that a stalking horse (a decoy) is found to help keep the process going in a positive direction.

On the very rare occasions, a financial deposit (may be non-refundable) can be requested by your broker at the time a potential buyer's offer is received. This is sometimes called 'earnest money', as it is designed to keep the buyer very interested and shows real commitment to completing the deal.

Performing Due Diligence

Due diligence is the part of the sale process that gives buyers the opportunity to make sure that they are buying what they are expecting and offers them assurance. This part of the process is controlled by your broker, and due diligence will be for a defined period of time. During this time, commercial, technical, operational, legal, and financial due diligence aspects will be carried out.

Due diligence is a two-way street and also gives you the chance to get to better know your potential buyer, as you will meet more people during conference calls and face-to-face meetings, and watch how they carry out due diligence on your business. Showing interest in how they operate and their people is going to provide more of an insight as to how similar or different each business' cultures are.

Having a squeaky clean, ordered business will help make this part of the sale process run smoothly. Otherwise, if you haven't spent time preparing, you may be giving a potential buyer a reason for reducing the consideration offered, also known as price chipping. But if you've read this book and addressed all aspects raised, the chances of being chipped should be greatly reduced.

Tip: Publicly listed companies on stock market exchanges will always carry out due diligence, it is part of their duties to their shareholders.

Solicitors may ask you to fill out a due diligence questionnaire (DDQ) document. This is used to help prepare the data room (the main due diligence tool), which will hold all the documentation relating to the business, from statutory accounts, to examples of product sales literature, to forecasts, and employee expenses policy—everything.

As well having the data room, due diligence will be carried out on physical property by visiting it, whether it's owned or leased by the business. This includes offices, warehouses, computer data centres, and retail shops.

Also, meetings will be requested to discuss your business's sales forecast, to understand your cost models in more depth and also to understand how products are developed and operations are undertaken.

Potential buyers will also want to talk to your top customers, to check on the fact that your business does provide products and services to them and to gauge what your client thinks of the business. This is handled delicately, and it is normally a reference request which happens very close to the end of the due diligence process, due to its sensitivity.

The structure of the data room is function based and covers financial, sales, marketing, HR, property deeds and leases, business and IT asset registers, contracts, acquisitions, financial accounts, cost models, statutory information, and management information.

Available on http://www.SellYourBusiness.biz/resources/free-document-samples is a sample data room structure.

On the website's store there is a more comprehensive 'Creating the Data Room Pack' which explains what a data room is, why its worth having data room software and what the charges are likely to be. The pack also includes a data room folder structure zip file, saving you time setting one up from scratch. Visit: http://www.SellYourBusiness.biz/store/products/creating-the-data-room-pack/

If you're selling to a larger organisation, the number of people involved will be numerous. Expect a large corporate organisation to have least 30 people in your data room. Don't let that put you off. It's just that corporate organisations can afford to have specialists, and it's also a tactic that potential buyers play to try and make you feel overwhelmed, which you won't be if you've completed all your preparations ahead of time.

I can't stress enough how much effort needs to go into preparing the contents of the data room *before* the management team presentations. Whatever date you thought to start, start one month earlier, ideally while the memorandum is being drafted or even before, because you're going to be busy meeting people, answering questions, and maintaining the day-to-day business too.

To help you get ready for due diligence we've created a Preparing for Due Diligence Checklist Pack available in the store which provides you with comprehensive checklists of what information will be requested.

And when you think your data room is ready, you can do a dry run through DD using our 'Due Diligence Questions Checklist Packs' which together contain over 500 questions that will make sure that you've definitely got all your bases covered. Just in case you're interested visit:

http://www.SellYourBusiness.biz/store/products/due-diligence-questions-checklist-pack-1 and measure exactly how ready your business' data room really is.

If you are worried about competition, don't be. In the data room, redacting (which means to edit and block out sensitive information) is a popular method to remove the sensitive parts of your data in the early stages, especially if it's a competitor who is going to be naturally curious about how you do something better than they do.

The entire contents of the data room will be included on Completion Day as part of the documentation. In the days before computers, this would have been photocopied or typed up duplicates of all documentation. These days, the solicitors will have all the information available on CDs/DVDs.

Everyone on your team will need access to the data room, and you may want to include your senior management team so that they can upload documents. This, of course, assumes that they have been brought into your confidence. The contents of the data room should be reviewed in whole by your financial advisor before the data room is officially opened. The solicitors can automatically upload the financial statutory information, as well as property information such as searches and lease.

The shortlisted potential buyers will be given a set period in which they will have access to the data room, and it is generally the financial advisor or solicitor that will grant access accordingly to the data room.

During the period that the data room is open, be prepared to update your data room information on a daily basis as a result of answering questions and as the business changes.

Tip: Have your company file server structure any information in the same format as your data room. It will save countless numbers of hours when you have to update the data room.

How to Handle Due Diligence Questions Efficiently and Effectively

During the due diligence process, a vast number of questions will be asked from each of the potential buyers. You may find that the same question gets asked over and over again, in different ways by different buyers. That's normal, and it is likely due to different people looking at the business from different functions.

Remember to only answer the question asked, don't expand on it. Never guess the answer, as everything is considered fact in the data room and contributes to your business' valuation.

To save you time and stay organised, there should be a spreadsheet for each potential buyer kept in separate folders in the data room, and this should include what the question was, who asked, and when they asked. Ideally, the answer will refer the reader to a data room item, or if it requires explanation, keep the answer concise.

To keep the due diligence process moving, your broker should set up weekly conference calls with key people from both sides of the negotiation table in order to check on progress, update all parties, and deal with any issues. On the call should be the lead brokers, solicitors, finance representative, yourself, and the main stakeholder from the potential buyer's side.

Receiving Best and Final Offers

During the due diligence process, your broker will encourage potential buyers to firm up their indicative offers and submit their best and final offers in writing directly to your broker, based on what they have checked in the data room, and encouraged by the other potential buyers in the process.

A potential buyers' best and final offer should include the request for exclusivity to be provided in order to complete due diligence, which also prevents you from receiving competing offers from other potential buyers during this time. Expect a completion date to be stated too, in order to encourage your broker to complete the deal with themselves. The offer letter may also state cancellation options (for example, if something of material significance is found during due diligence). Finally, the letter may also include more details on the terms of the earn-out, if applicable.

If you don't like or are disappointed by a potential buyer's best and final offer, you could let them know by way of your broker by giving them a chance to address the areas of concern. However, be aware that deal fever may be affecting decisions.

If you accept a potential buyer's offer, the next step is for both you and the buyer to sign the letter that reflects the agreement reached, which signifies agreement to the purchase offer and all its terms and conditions.

Getting to Completion Day

This is the day when the paperwork is all signed and the ownership of the company changes hands in exchange for the agreed Consideration. You will remember this date forever.

Although generally referred to as 'Completion Day', actual completion could be longer than a day. The 'day' is normally a day in the working week. Friday seems to be popular as the weekend can be used as a negotiation tactic, but it has the potential to be a lovely ending to a hard working week.

Getting everyone to the Completion Day shows that both parties want to do the deal. But it's not a guarantee that you will complete. Don't assume because you've got to the day itself that it's a done deal. Remember those chickens? They haven't hatched yet. In fact, you are still negotiating. The completion date will change so expect turns, twists, and potential delays.

If you want to know if Completion Day will go ahead or not, very simply follow the money trail. Completion Day cannot take place if the funds are not held by the buyers' solicitors. Completion Day may not even take place until the funds are transferred to the sellers' (that's your) solicitors.

Drawing up the Sale and Purchase Agreement

The sale and purchase agreement (SPA) is the official legal document prepared by your solicitors in order to complete the sale. The agreement will easily run to over 100 pages and be full of legalese.

The SPA may be readied in advance of the first opening day of the data room, as both your Corporate Advisor and solicitor will ask the potential buyer to use their prepared SPA. However, it is likely that the buyer will want to use their own which is generally deferred to.

If the potential buyers start looking at the SPA early, while due diligence is progressing, it indicates commitment on their part and seriousness in wanting to purchase your business, especially as they will be paying professional fees to their solicitors.

Expect a couple of dedicated meetings to page turn through the SPA. It is important that you read through the document and double check the details, as you may pick up on something the advisors haven't yet.

As part of preparing for completion, minority sellers will be asked to sign their stock transfer forms in advance, to negate the need of all shareholders being present on Completion Day.

What goes into the disclosure letter?

The disclosure letter process is owned by the solicitors, however it requires input from the business itself as it will contain everything that you declare and forms an important part of the sale documentation. It will include items such as reference to data room items, recent pay rises, director drawings, references to exceptional items, large capital equipment purchases, acquisitions, and especially things that haven't been done that should have e.g. portable appliance tests (PAT testing).

If you leave something out of the disclosure letter that is deemed to be 'something big' and it is discovered later on, it could trigger a warranty payout back to the buyer. You don't want to be in the position of handing back cash (especially if you've already spent it), so it is better to be upfront as much as possible so that there are no future and costly surprises in store for either party.

To see what a disclosure letter actually looks like, there's one available in Sell Your Business website's Free Documents Samples section:

http://www.SellYourBusiness.biz/resources/free-document-samples

Have you checked your new service contract?

If you are staying on in the business post completion, you will have a new service contract that you will need to sign as part of the Completion Day paperwork. Make sure that you have a specialist employment lawyer check over the details before agreeing to the service contract.

TIP: Your new service contract will not cover the terms of your earn-out (if applicable) as the earn-out forms part of the SPA.

What happens during Completion Day?

To give you an idea here's the ideal 'what happens' during Completion day. Normally, everyone converges on the buyers' solicitors' offices early in the day. And by everyone, that includes your team, yourself, any other shareholders that need to sign (unless power of attorney has been given), your corporate finance advisor should be present, your solicitor and their associates, as well as the potential buyer's team.

Expect at least three rooms to be put aside with a couple spare. Here is how they are normally used:

Signing Room

This is where all the paperwork will be laid out in order of signature. Just to give you an idea, 30 piles of paperwork is considered to be a small, simple deal, but other deals may require a larger conference table or a couple of signing rooms!

Buyer's Room

This is where the buyer's team makes camp, though they will have their own offices and resources to call upon if needed.

Seller's Room

This is where you and your team make camp

Negotiation Room 1

This is where buyer and seller representatives, normally your corporate financial advisor with the acquisitions manager, or people leading the seller's team, meet for negotiation chats.

Negotiation Room 2

This room is reserved just in case private conversations with members of your team need to be held. This could be due to a negotiation point that your corporate financial advisor wants to discuss with you, or this could be your solicitor wanting to have your input on some of the legal paperwork, like the disclosure letter.

Once the last points have been successfully negotiated, the solicitors frantically make the last set of changes to all the legal paperwork and review each other's work.

If the buyers' solicitors haven't yet transferred the cash to the bank account of the sellers' solicitors, this must happen before the banking transfer cut off time.

At the appointed time, when both sides' solicitors are ready, everyone is ushered into the signing room where all the legal documentation is laid out including:

- Your business's statutory books, registers, and records (company minutes book, seal, Articles of Association, and Memorandum of Association)
- Company certificate of registration
- Share certificates
- Bank mandates
- SPA
- Disclosure letter, deeds, and warranties
- Service contract (if applicable)

Each party's solicitors take turns in checking and signing all the paperwork - this bit could take hours, depending on the complexity of the deal. There could also be other parties in other rooms that are part of the overall deal (e.g. two venture capital firms are joining while one exits).

As part of the completion process, you may be asked by the buyer to resign from being a company director, and have your signatory and access to the bank revoked as a precautionary measure.

With your pen at the ready, sign where indicated by your solicitors. By the time your hand hurts from all that signing, hopefully, the end is near, which will be confirmed by the solicitors officially giving each other the nod and saying the magical words 'We have completed.'

WOOHOO! At this point, a lot of handshaking takes place, congratulations are offered all around, and the champagne starts flowing.

It all sounds real simple but Completion Days rarely are anything but! It's worth preparing yourself for it and I've created 'The Seller's Completion Day Checklist Pack' to help you do exactly that. It's something that I wished I had so I knew what to expect on the day and how to get through the tough moments during the course of Completion Day. You can find it in our store here:

http://www.SellYourBusiness.biz/store/products/the-sellers-completion-day-checklist-pack/

The After Party!

Congratulations on crossing the finish line! You've made it. You're probably exhausted and still shell shocked from having actually crossed the finish line. Take a deep breath, savour and enjoy the moment of euphoria, and hold onto that feeling.

Depending on the terms of your deal, your sales process may be ongoing due to an agreed earn-out and future promises that will need to be delivered on, or you may have agreed to stay on during the handover period. Regardless of what the situation is going to be, take a moment and enjoy it. Celebrate! You've earned it and more.

Ideally, going to market and closing the deal is going to be a smooth, single, sales cycle for you, and I wish you and your team all the success in your endeavour. What I can promise is that your business sale process is going to be unique. There is so much that can happen while you're engaged in the business sale process that unless you've been told about it from someone who's been through the experience, like myself, or experienced it yourself before, there is so much unknown. The following section covers specific situations or scenarios that I and my business partner came across, which I am sure will be of use to you, as it's aimed to reduce the amount of guess work and unwelcome surprises during the business sale process. It will help you either avoid the situation, or you will make the most of the situation.

Part Five – How Many Business Sale Tips and Tricks Do You Know?

Dealing with Unsolicited Approaches

On occasion, you may be approached, either directly or via a third party, expressing interest in your business and seemingly wanting to purchase it. It's happened to me. It's very flattering and nice to be approached, regardless of the final outcome. When it happened to me, it turned out to be a red herring and a small distraction for the business, as it caught my business partner and I off guard at the time.

By all means, entertain the idea and quickly find out if they can really afford to buy your business or if it is just a speculative play to see if you would bite at the opportunity. Remember, if you decide to pursue it, it's always better to have more than one party interested in your business as it creates scarcity. With scarcity, a bidding war can ensue, allowing the value of your business to increase.

If you're halfway through grooming your business, you could let the interested party know you're not considering options at this time, but promise to contact them in the future if and when you're ready to go to market.

How do I manage all the shareholders?

You may be the sole shareholder owning 100% of your business. Well done and lucky you, as there's only you to manage!

If you have a number of shareholders in the business, make sure that you have a *signed* shareholders agreement which covers what happens in the event of a sale. For example, most shareholder agreements will have what's known as a 'drag and tag along' clause, which protects the interests of the majority shareholder. So, should the majority shareholders sell their stake, the minority shareholders will have to sell too, usually at the same price and terms, as minority shareholders do not have any another option available to them.

Minimising the Risks to Potential Buyers

All businesses have associated risks. The trick is to make sure that they are managed correctly during the business sale process. During the due diligence process, a number of risks will show up. As long as you can mitigate them, you will be fine, and the potential buyer will be unable to use the discovered risks against you during negotiations to maximum effect, which would in turn devalue your valuation.

For example, if your business has a small client list, make sure that all contracts are signed, have good contract length and a long termination clause (3 months is better than 1 month), your sales pipeline forecast looks strong, and the conversion rate is high. If you have a high staff turnover, this could be explained (if true) that it's a result of you replacing your non-productive staff members.

Loving Your Customers More

Hopefully, you already love your customers, and closing new business is already being greatly helped by existing customer referrals. If your business hasn't done so already, start cultivating relationships with individuals within your customer base. Target ones that would be great advocates for your business. It doesn't have to be you personally, and in fact, it's better that it's not you and part of account management. If you're wondering why, it's worth it because during due diligence you will be asked for a list of customers the potential buyer will call to discuss what that customer thinks about your business products, services, and customer relations.

TIP: If a customer has recently left the business, don't burn any bridges. Instead, keep in touch with regular contact, as you will most likely be asked by the potential buyer for this type of customer reference too.

Maintaining Confidentiality During the Business Sale Process

Keeping a lid on the fact your business is on the market for sale is a challenge, but here are a few ideas I used that will help you too.

1. **Have potential buyers sign an NDA**

   Make sure all potential buyers sign a confidentiality agreement (the NDA), before any specific company details are provided. Explain clearly why confidentiality in this process is absolutely necessary and that you will keep any information that they give you confidential as well.

2. **Keep your company number private**

   Do not give out your landline number, especially if it happens to be the company switchboard number. You don't want the employee who answers the phone to become concerned. Only give out and use your mobile/cell phone number during the business sale process.

3. **Set up a private email address**

   Do not use your work email address for any activities related to the business sale. Setup and use a private email address that no-one else in the business has access to.

4. **Use your home address**

   If anything needs to be mailed to you to you, use your home address. If it has to go to the office, 'private and confidential' isn't necessarily going to prevent someone else from opening up post addressed to you, especially if your secretary is aware of the ongoing business sale process.

5. **Use a private calendar**

   Be very careful with putting your meetings in your public calendar (and the company calendar if there is one). Remember, others can read who and where you're meeting. Best to refer to businesses you would like to partner or are exploring opportunities with, and leave out names and locations. Book the time off as holiday instead.

6. **Have a good cover story**

   Have a good cover story for employees who may suspect something is up. Keeping it close to the truth and keeping the story simple will go a long way. If they bluntly ask 'Are you selling?', have your sarcastic reply ready: 'Of course! If the price is right, and it has lots of zeros at the end, why not? Are you offering to buy?'

When should we go out to market?

When deciding on when to go out to market, take into consideration seasonal periods. November is not ideal, as its right before the start of the Christmas period and close to the new year. Starting in July is leading right into the quiet month of August, as everyone is on holiday. I recommend starting in the second week of January, that's when my business partner and I started, and the third time around we started in late September, which slowed right down as we were waiting for an offer over Christmas, which had us distracted from our families.

How long will it take to find the right buyer?

There is no rule of thumb for how long it takes to find a buyer. It will depend on a number of factors, such as market demand, which companies can afford to purchase your business, their interest, and how well your business is marketed.

You may be one of the lucky ones and find a buyer to whom you do end up selling the business to within one year. It may take longer, as the market isn't ready in terms of potential buyers, or the price at which they buy at is lower than your walkaway price.

Sell, sell, sell!

Remember you are in selling mode—always. Don't forget this, as it could reduce your valuation.

With new market entrants or those organisations that want to set up a new division in your space, you'll find that you spend most of your time educating them and demonstrating how you operate commercially. It's a harder sell. How badly they want your business will make it easier so find out what the driving factors are behind their interest. Do they have an acquisition fund chest to spend within the year? Did their CEO publicly declare they were entering the market next year? Are you in the way of something that they want? (This is a good thing.) Is your business something they simply must have at all costs?

A word of caution: potential buyers are not your friends. You are not sitting on the same side of the table, at least not yet. Remember to show your best side on all occasions, whether in a formal setting in a meeting room, or informal having dinner together, and remember you are building up a relationship with potential future colleagues.

Reputation Matters

You may find that your business reputation precedes you going out to market, that's good as long as your business is being talked about in glowing terms. To make sure that this is likely to happen invest the time in loving your customers and turning them into advocates, that's a function of account management and is very important.

If your business' reputation in the market isn't that great, find out why. It may just be a couple of clients or individuals spreading the negativity. Try to get to the nub of the issue and solve it, especially if it's happening in one of your key client accounts. At the very least, try to change the person's viewpoint to be neutral, the best case would be turning them into advocates as they are most likely to rave about your business even more.

A great reputation is priceless as it can help keep buyers at the table or bring them back. This happened to a friend of mine, he was selling his business and the buyer went away and everywhere they went, the business name cropped up with positive terms and the buyer came back to the negotiation table! And in case you're wondering, there was a happy ending as my friend successfully sold to that same buyer.

How to Maintain Tension and Focus

Corporate finance advisors and brokers like using the word 'tension' during the sale process, which is directed at the potential buyers and the tension between them, so that sale process can progress and give the seller an edge during the negotiations as interested parties are more likely to present their best offers when they know there are others in the running.

Make sure you respond to potential buyers quickly and be transparent.

If you can help it, never have a sole interested potential buyer. They can sniff this off from miles away and will play on it because they know you have nowhere to go. Try having a stalking horse (a decoy) which will encourage potential buyers to progress their negotiations and keep true.

How to Agree on Your Walkaway Price

A walkaway price is exactly what it conveys. If the price offered is lower than your walkaway price, politely get up from that negotiation table, grab your jacket or handbag, and walk away. More easily said than done we know, but it's worth it as there will always be another deal to be had.

And in hindsight this was one of the best pieces of advice ever given to me, so get ready to set your minimum acceptable price for the business on completion *before* starting the sale process and before looking for a buyer.

The reason your walkaway price should be set now instead of later is this is as rational as you could possibly be before being carried away by the sale process. And, yes, you will be carried away at some point during the sale process with deal fever, that's a guarantee.

The walkaway (a.k.a. minimum acceptable) price must be a pure *cash* figure which you receive into your bank account when you sign and complete the Sale Purchase Agreement. The rest, be it shares or earn out incentives, may have value associated with it, but there is a chance it will not be realised. Do you have your pen and paper ready yet? Make time now, this is crucial planning. Spend *at least* 20 minutes on this.

Write down a cash figure down now.

Did you write down a range instead of just one figure? We're looking for a single figure. And remember, it's cash only. If you're having difficulties quantifying it in financial terms, how about starting by writing down how and where you would spend the money, and add it all up. Here's an example:

Pay off house mortgage:	£340,000
Private schooling for 5 years:	£100,000
Invest for a rainy day (pension):	£500,000
Buy a fancy car:	£100,000
What I believe the business is worth:	£500,000

Total walkaway cash price: £1,540,000.

Now give it a go. Are you sure your list is accurate enough and complete? Are there any expenses you missed?

Let's make sure you've covered everything, as there is actually something big missing from the above list which will become clear when we look at it another way. Name a figure and break it down backwards. Here's another example:

Aim: Sell for £3 million cash on completion.

Deduct professional advisors fees:	£150,000
Deduct Employee Share Scheme:	£ 50,000
Deduct company loan(s) redemption:	£500,000
Deduct tax (@ 10% Entrepreneur's Relief):	£300,000

Approximate net: £2m cash

(This example ignores excess cash in the business.)

Surprised to see that initial figure being eaten away? Selling is an expensive business in both time and money.

Are you sure about that price? How many times did you scribble a figure out and replace it with another? Bet you it went up, not down.

Now you've got your figure, write down your walkaway cash price in indelible ink, date it, and keep it somewhere safe and accessible. List the top three reasons for justifying your walkaway price. Spend time on these reasons, because these are going to comfort you when you receive an offer that is lower. Take time to think it over. Leave it be a couple of days and come back to it. Are the price tag and reasons still valid? Does it hold after further scrutiny? If not, adjust it accordingly by writing out the new figure and its three reasons. Don't forget to date it. Keep it all as a record.

Of course, at any time, you can always come back and change the figure, but you have been warned. That's risky, as you will be in the midst of deal fever and influenced by recent events. Thinking straight and objectively will be hard. That's why you list your reasons: to remind you why you set the figure as you did.

If you need help calculating your walkaway price check out the website store at **SellYourBuziness.biz** as you'll find our 'Calculate Your Walkaway Price Pack' there.

How to Say No to Potential Buyers

You are entirely within your rights to say no to a potential buyer if you don't like their offer and it appears a deal cannot be reached between both parties at any point during your business sale process. However, it's essential that when you do so, you do it correctly. Here are some tips to saying no the right way:

1. Express regret

When you say no, don't forget to express your regret that you are not in the position to continue with the potential buyer at the present time.

2. State the reasons why you cannot continue at this time clearly

You don't want your potential buyer walking away confused. Clearly and concisely, let them know why you feel that they aren't the best fit at the present time. Remain kind, and choose your words carefully.

3. End the meeting on a positive note

Make sure that you end on a positive note. Be polite, and thank them sincerely for their time. Ask them to keep your contact information, and let them know that you will be doing the same with theirs.

4. Leave a window open

The door may be closed at this particular time, but you never know which way the wind is going to blow. Leave a window open for future communication. As time moves on, everything can be reconsidered, even the points that resulted in stalemate at the time.

Potential buyers, even if they aren't the right fit now, may also have the ability to become a part of your extended network. They may know someone else who is a better fit, or in the future, they may be able to benefit your business in another way. In business, never burn bridges. You can never be certain where they might lead.

How to Manage Non-performing Employees

Now is also the time to manage non-performing employees out of your business, if you haven't done so already. Everyone in the business needs to be pulling their weight and contributing to the business results. If an employee is a drain on the business, they are dragging your numbers down, which means your numbers aren't as good as they can be for the valuation. To manage non-performing people, make sure that your appraisal system is in place and working, and follow your formally documented disciplinary procedures. You can also, of course, make employees redundancies that need to follow certain procedures, depending on the size of your business.

An alternative way to let a non-performing employee go is to use a Compromise Agreement, which is where an employer offers an employee a consideration, often a negotiated financial sum, in exchange for agreeing that he or she will have no further claim against the employer as a result of any breach of a statutory obligation by the employer. However, before embarking on this course of action, seek the advice of an HR specialist.

How to Help Your Staff if the Buyer Is Going to Let Them All Go

If you strongly believe your staff will be let go, you could increase their notice periods from one to two months as part of a review of all employee contracts. This should be done as early as possible while preparing the business for sale. Applying an increased notice period across the board will be fair to everyone and easy to justify the reason for doing so, to all employees.

Alternatively, during the sale negotiations and assuming that there is no earn-out, you could negotiate to have certain employees excluded from your restrictive covenants, thereby placing you in a position to hire them should the right opportunity arise post sale.

How to Cope with Potential Buyers Visiting Your Premises

When potential buyers visit your premises, make sure there's a realistic cover story, just in case your staff wonder who the visitors are. It could be your visitors are looking for partnership, a potential customer is carrying out an audit, or you've agreed to help them with your business' operational best practices.

TIP: If your visitors have to sign in, ask the visitors to use a different and/or fake company name and only give their first name at reception. This protects you against your staff doing a LinkedIn search and finding out who the visitors really are! This also protects you from other potential buyers who may be visiting afterwards, as they will definitely look through the visitor record book for clues.

Business Records You Need to Keep

It's vital to know the business records that you need to keep so that when it comes time to sell your business, all records are current and ready to go. Depending on the size of your business, this will more than likely not be something that you will do yourself. Delegate. Delegate. Delegate. Hire someone that you trust to handle the financial records, and then check in to make sure that they are being held accountable. If they are doing their job, you won't have to spend a great deal of time crunching numbers or sorting through piles of files. Everything will already be well-organised and clear for you and/or your potential buyer to review.

The following are the business records that you need to make sure someone is managing properly at all times:

1. **Sales**

   Know what has been coming in, and know what has been going out. Make sure receipts are being kept in order. Make sure that invoices are being dealt with properly. Have good credit control and make sure that clients are paying on time and that all outstanding invoices get paid.

2. **Expenses**

   Make sure that your business has an account of its own. Many small business owners use their private accounts when starting a business. This can lead to disaster when selling your business. Open a separate business account, use it for business matters and business matters only, and keep track of all purchases. Receipts need to be saved, dated, and amounts kept as part of the record keeping.

3. **Inventory**

   Anything you purchase with the intent to resell would be considered your inventory. How much you purchased the items for and how much you sell them for must be carefully documented and all receipts and invoices dated and saved.

4. **Assets**

   How much did you purchase them for? Was any maintenance necessary on your assets? These are expenses that must be watched carefully, because they are subject to depreciation. Keep receipts and make sure they are clearly dated.

You may feel a bit overwhelmed at the thought of keeping boxes and filing cabinets full of receipts. In this technology age, that is no longer necessary. Scan receipts. Save invoices onto the computer. Have everything organised and dated properly. Above all, delegate to other trusted sources when possible.

Understanding the Data Room Software and Its Charges

These days, software is used to manage the data room virtually, which has made the job of having a data room so much easier, and it is a great time saver. Data room software is worth it, as file storage providers such as Dropbox and Box.net don't provide all the features, which I'll cover below.

Data room software allows you to upload documents in a structured way, and it will automatically provide a full audit trail of when the document was updated and by whom. It also allows you to review the changes before committing them and making it public. User and group permissions form a very important part, as it controls access to parts of the data room and can restrict documents so that they can only be viewed online in supported web browsers and can't be printed (in full, unless someone is going to sit there and patiently screen grab every page).

There is also a comprehensive set of reports available which report on who has looked at which document, who last logged in, and when documents were last updated.

Either your solicitor or financial advisor will recommend a data room software to use, generally based on their own experience, and there will be charges for using data room software, which is normally invoiced to your solicitor on your behalf so that the charges don't raise any questions with your day-to-day business financial team.

The charges are normally based on per document upload, and each time a document is viewed, charges may run into the thousands, depending on how many potential buyers you have in the data room.

Understanding What a Deed of Contribution Is For

If there is more than one seller (multiple shareholders), the sellers have to provide guarantees and either be individually or collectively liable in the case of a breach of warranty.

Where there are multiple sellers, warranties can be given either jointly or 'jointly and severally'.

Joint and several liability for warranties means each seller assumes the obligation for the accuracy of the warranties both collectively (i.e., on behalf of each of the other sellers) and also individually. If, following completion of the sale and purchase, the buyer decides to bring a claim for breach of warranty, this claim can either be brought against all the sellers collectively or against one of the sellers individually. The buyer can claim in full against one of the sellers for the full amount of the claim, even if the amount claimed is more than the split of the consideration that seller actually received or if another seller caused the breach in question

If the sellers must accept joint and several liability (due to a lack of bargaining strength), then they may consider entering into a deed of contribution at completion. If the buyer subsequently brought a claim against one of the sellers, under such a deed that seller would have the right to seek a contribution from the other sellers. This is useful as it protects the position of minority shareholders.

Limiting SPA Liabilities

As a seller, your solicitor should always seek for the sale and purchase agreement to provide for individual caps on liability. For example, if the total consideration is £1,000,000, which is to be split equally between 4 sellers, the maximum liability of each individual seller should be capped at £250,000. Normally, the cap split is determined as per the shareholding percentages held.

Pre-Completion Day Checklist

The night before, get a very good night's sleep. Having gone through it myself, I know it's tough to keep cool, calm, and collected, as you're so close to the finish line and excited that Competition Day is the next day. The following are some tips to keep in mind:

1. **Understand that Completion Day may be a very long day**
   Plan accordingly the night before, and pack an overnight bag, just in case Completion Day extends into more than just one day. Make sure that you have all of your essentials packed and ready to go the night before so that all you have to do the morning of Completion Day is wake up refreshed, eat a healthy breakfast, and arrive at the meeting on time.

2. **Pack healthy food and water**
   Make sure that you have some energy food at the ready too. Some blueberries or raw almonds can both be a good choice. Leave the garlic salmon sandwich at home. Healthy and energising? Yes. Do you want to be the stinky seller? No. Make sure that you DO NOT skip any meals. Also, make sure you have water; staying hydrated is a

must for remaining alert. Stay away from coffee if possible. It will give you short bursts of energy, but once it wears off, your alertness level will decline.

3. **Bring your notebook**

A great way to pass the time, when there are lulls, is to bring a notebook and jot down ideas of what you'd like to do when the sale is over. Do you want to go on vacation somewhere? Plan out where you'd like to go, who you want to go with, and what activities you'd like to do once there. Or, another idea would be to get started on writing your thank-you notes to those who have helped you get to where you are now. When was the last time you received a hand-written thank-you note instead of a text or email? The extra time and thought of a hand-written note will be greatly appreciated.

4. **Bring some entertainment**

There may be some downtime. Bring a book that you've wanted to read for awhile, or a pack a few travel magazines so that you can research your vacation location. Or, at the very least, download the latest version of the Temple Run app onto your phone; that should keep you busy for awhile! Just make sure you keep the sound off; wouldn't want you looking unprofessional, now.

5. **Don't forget to say, "Cheese!"**

Make sure that you remember to bring your camera. This is a day you'll want to remember!

6. **Get ready to sign, sign, sign**

Make sure that you have a few nice pens, full of ink, so that you are ready to sign all the documents. The last thing you want to happen is for it to be time to sign on the dotted line and have a poor quality pen or to have to ask the buyer to borrow one of theirs. Be prepared.

7. **Stay positive**
   Don't underestimate the power of a positive attitude. Stay calm and collected. If you've done what you're supposed to ahead of time, you're ready for this!

Completion Day Negotiation Tactics

Expect final negotiations and discussions to take place while the solicitors are still thrashing out changes to the SPA, warranties, and deeds. This is normal practice and everything happens in parallel during the day.

If the funds are being held by the buyers' solicitors, be aware that the funds have to move by a certain cut off time (3pm in the UK for a CHAPS transfer), and if transferring in from abroad from a different currency, this could take even more time. This can be used as a negotiation point. 'If we can't agree on the deal before 3pm, the funds won't be transferred in time, so we can't do the deal until tomorrow, Monday, or not at all.'

If the funds are with your solicitors and negotiations are still happening past 4pm, don't worry, this is fine, and the solicitors will have their own overnight bags at the ready and are prepared to work through the night if needed.

You may find that as everyone gets more tired, a break is called, which might be the weekend. This is particularly hard emotionally, as the uncertainly will gnaw at you. But don't forget the other party will be having the similar feelings. They have invested both emotionally and financially to get to this point. Sensible heads should prevail and hold steady through this period of unknown. Use the time to go do something different, play a round of golf, go to a spa, or sleep through the weekend. Relax and keep your mind busy, away from over thinking about the deal.

Where's my money?

You may have expected the cash to be in your bank account on Completion Day. But actually that's not the case, and if you're an Englishman, you may have been too polite at the time.

Any cash element of the deal will be transferred to your bank account days later by your solicitors, and that's after the expenses relating to the sale have been paid for. So, it is in your best interest to encourage your solicitor to get on with this part of the process!

Your solicitors will draw up a list of expenses that relate to the sale from all the invoices received, and will be responsible for paying all the parties (including themselves) directly after receiving your permission to do so.

Your solicitors may also, at the shareholder's request, continue to hold funds in escrow (which refers to money held by a third party on behalf of transacting parties) to cover warranties and other agreed actions between both parties as part of the sale purchase agreement. These escrow funds can be released at a later date with the shareholders permission.

TIP: Make sure to check with your solicitor that these escrow funds are earning interest, which accrues to shareholders in their shareholding proportions.

Your solicitors will also calculate what percentage of the sale funds is due to each shareholder, and once the calculation has been reviewed and approved by the shareholders (at least the majority shareholder), the funds will be transferred to your nominated bank account.

Expect to receive your cash at least 10 days after Completion Day. When you receive it, take a snapshot of your bank account balance and smile broadly.

The Importance of Thanking Everyone

You're coming to the end of your business-selling journey. It's now time to thank those who have gotten you to the place you are now. A little bit of appreciation can go a very, very long way. The following are some examples of who you need to thank and how:

1. **Your Staff**

   While you were busy selling the business, your staff have been keeping the home fires burning and kept busy making sure that business continued to performed. Acknowledge this publicly. Take them all out on a social event, a trip into London to the theatre and a fancy dinner. Give them each a case of wine, write individual thank you cards and highlight something in particular that they did. They will feel appreciated and hopefully be keen to help you going forward and if you were to start a new venture they might want to join!

2. **Your Business Sale Team**

They have helped you get the business successfully sold. Don't begrudge them their fees, they have earned it. Take the time to thank them. Make sure that they know you appreciate everything that they have done for you. You might be using them again in future!

3. **Your Secretary**

S/he often times gets to work even before you do. The coffee she has ready for you at your desk when you arrive in your office is always hot, fresh, and with two creams and 1 sugar—just the way you like it. Your voicemail messages have been set next to the coffee arranged in order of importance, and your important emails have been flagged or printed out for you to review. All of that didn't just magically appear. Your secretary has been hard at work, making sure that your office is running smoothly and efficiently. For a nice surprise, arrive at work before she does, and have a gift basket waiting for her with a hand-written thank-you note. As an added bonus, you could also have a nice, hot cup of coffee waiting, just the way she likes it.

4. **Your Home Partner**

He's been by your side. He's made dinner for the kids when you have to work late, and he's packed the kids' lunches. He's your support, your right-hand man, and he deserves a big thank you. Plan a romantic getaway for just the two of you. Perhaps choose a quiet little bed-and-breakfast inn or a quiet cabin away from the hustle and bustle of daily life. It doesn't necessarily have to be fancy, but it does have to be romantic. Once there, genuinely express to the love of your life that you don't take a thing that he's done for granted.

5. **Your Children**

   They haven't seen you a lot lately, and they've missed you. They have understood when you have to unexpectedly have to work late, and they have been quiet when an important phone call comes in. Take them to the park, fly kites, and have some fun. If it's in the budget, plan a kid-fun vacation. Go to Disneyland, or go to a waterpark. Tell them you are thankful for how good they have been while you've been working so much lately.

6. **Your Buyer**

   This has been quite the process, and they have been with you throughout. Meeting after meeting, phone call after phone call, the endless amount of emails and texts, they are troupers, too! After all is said and done, send a note expressing your gratitude. Ask them if they'd like to meet for lunch sometime. Send a gift basket congratulating them on their new business.

Without all of the above people, your success would not have been possible.

You should never underestimate how far an attitude of gratitude can take you. You are not an island; you have reached this point in your life because you have a support system surrounding you and walking alongside you. Take a moment to appreciate the people in your life that help you in many ways, both big and small.

What Shall I Do Now?

Realistically, after hitting an emotional high at the point of signing, you are probably on an emotional low. Allow it to happen. It's only natural, and you may not want to celebrate. But, you must! Here are some ideas to get you started.

1. **Take a long holiday**

   Stop thinking about work for a while. You deserve the time to kick back and relax. Do something you've always wanted to (keep it legal), and spend some of that hard-earned cash that's sitting in your bank account. Have a crazy moment, and get it out of your system. Otherwise, it could build up over time and wreak havoc. Go somewhere that you've always dreamed of going. Relax on the beach in Fiji. Go skiing in Switzerland. Try backpacking in Spain. Party with friends in Vegas! You know what you want to do, so go and do it.

2. **Splurge on something special**

   Perhaps purchase something that will last longer than a dinner or holiday. How about a piece of artwork or a nice timepiece? Buy yourself something special. Every time you look at it, it can be a good reminder, and you can feel proud of all the hard work you've done.

3. **Make some time for yourself**

   Now is the time to take a deep breath, and do a mental health check. Your brain has been spinning non-stop, and your body has been go-go-going. Plan a day at the spa, and get a massage. Turn off your phone. Do not check your email. RELAX. Breathe in. Breath out...in...out...

4. **Spend some time with your family**

   You've been busy. You've been distracted. You've been working many, many late nights on the business sale process. That's over now. Take the time to reconnect with your partner and children. Take the kids to the park and out to get an ice cream. Take your partner horseback riding and wine tasting. Listen to what's been going on in their lives and reconnect. They've missed you.

5. **Be responsible**

   Now is the time to de-risk a little and look after yourself and the family. If you don't plan on moving homes, consider paying off the mortgage and other debts you may have. A great deal of stress is associated with debt. De-stress yourself, and eliminate as much debt as possible.

6. **Keep the taxman happy**

   Don't spend or risk the money earmarked for paying tax. Put it away or pay off the taxman early; that's one less important thing you have to worry about.

And if your solicitors are holding funds in escrow for warranties, treat the funds as untouchable until the appropriate amount of time has passed, which could be years after the Completion Day, until the buyer has no recourse to claim back any post sale liabilities found.

Announcing Your Successful Sale

As part of the business transaction deal, you may have already agreed on a communications plan, and you may have agreed that the consideration amount would not be announced (this can only happen with private companies, listed companies have to announce the financial terms of the deal).

The communications plan should address what medium should be used, how, when and where the news will be announced and to whom. The plan should be different depending on the audience type, for example:

- The purchased business's staff (your ex-business)
- The Buyer's staff
- The purchased business's clients
- The purchased business's suppliers
- The market as a whole

If this plan hasn't yet been agreed, it's worth mentioning it before Completion Day and getting the details right.

There is also the tricky situation about how you are going to tell your close work colleagues, friends and family and whether or not you're going to tell people the amount you sold for. Believe me, it's harder than you think not to say anything because in a way you're proud of your achievement and want to share the news. It really depends on how comfortable you are with broadcasting your news and the amounts involved. Everyone will assume that the successful sale will have made you a multi-millionaire, this might be true but they aren't going to really know unless you tell them or your lifestyle changes to match that of a multi-millionaire.

I dealt with this tricky situation by simply not telling anyone for months and then decided to drip feed the 'old news' to a couple close friends at time and it slowly made the rounds so the ripple effect was small instead of waves. Personally, I chose not to state the amount and blamed the legal paperwork for having to keep mum about it, so far that's worked for me!

A Quick Word on Earn-outs

Based on my personal observations so far, earn-outs are more likely to happen if the buyer is a public company or a venture capital company. They are difficult beasts to define, let alone successfully manage. Earn-outs are likely to tie you to the business for a couple of years, and ideally you want to be given the opportunity to state your own earn-out terms. When you do, keep it simple and make sure you've considered your role in the organisation. To come up with effective earn-out measurements, knowing what the new owner's longer-term plan will be would be mightily handy, but you might not be privy to it yet.

If you're staying on in the business and have an earn-out, depending on what has been negotiated, be prepared to earn a lower basic salary to what you've been used to. The purchaser will have considered they have paid you enough on completion, so why should they continue to do so now you have all the money!

During your earn-out period, focus on how you ensure that you maximise your earn-out payout while you're not the owner of the business anymore. That's going to be tough to do, because you'll still care. Nothing else other than your earn-out and how you can get it matters. Really, it doesn't. Sure, be excited that you are working with new people and can see the opportunities and believe in the bigger picture, but don't get distracted, especially when the success of your earn-out results in more cash in your own pocket.

If you do have an earn-out, bear in mind that you have the power to negotiate costs out of the numbers, even post-sale, so if your employer (or the parent company) wants you to invest in something that might be counter to you achieving your earn out, you can ask them to 'normalise' it.

One beauty about earn-outs is, post-sale, if the combined entity is sold, your earn-out will cash out at its maximum value. That clause should definitely be included in the SPA, so if you think the combined entity is going to be flipped (sold again), that's going to work to your advantage.

Understanding Restrictive Covenants in the SPA

When you sell your business, the buyer will want certain guarantees, as the last thing they want is for you to be free to set up a competing business that could reduce their return on investment. Covenant clauses will include the following:

- Not being able to poach clients away from the business for a set duration
- Not being able to offer staff members, especially senior management team members, employment
- Not to setup a new business or compete in the same market for a set period e.g. 3 years is average, with 5 years becoming the normal and geographic location e.g. Global or United Kingdom only or English primary speaking countries only

If you have an earn-out, the non-compete could include future products and services the business has yet to offer. This is used to encourage you to stay and help the organisation.

Understanding What the 'Locked Box' Mechanism Is

The 'locked box' mechanism is when the buyer and seller agree on a fixed purchase price, where no changes will be made to the purchase price after completion of the transaction.

The purchase price is calculated based on a balance sheet (this is the locked box) at a date agreed between the buyer and the seller, before finalising the share purchase agreement. The balance sheet doesn't necessarily need to be the audited balance sheet. Ideally, the locked box balance sheet should be drawn up fairly close to the signing of the share purchase agreement. A buyer will then determine the purchase price, based on the locked box balance sheet, taking into account your business's cash/debt position and working capital. Once the seller has accepted the purchase price offered by the buyer, this becomes the purchase price in the share purchase agreement and becomes the amount payable by the buyer at completion.

The major advantage with the locked box mechanism is it saves time and money for both parties, as there is no need for adjustment or determination of the purchase price after completion of the transaction.

A disadvantage of the locked box mechanism is it requires heavier warranties and indemnities to be negotiated in relation to the locked box balance sheet, and the net indebtedness of the target, as well as substantial warranties and covenants to protect the buyer against leakage of value from the company. Some leakage examples are:

- That your business won't suddenly have a large capital expenditure invoice.
- That your business will not make any dividends or other distributions to its shareholders.
- That your business won't make any extraordinary payment to the seller, its affiliates, or management.

Expect the Unexpected

Expect deal fever, it's guaranteed to happen, after all we are only human, and it is your company you're selling and very tempting monetary figures are placed in front of you. The symptoms of deal fever are trying to rationalise and re-rationalise decisions and choices made. It's changing your mind a thousand times. It's thinking about the 'what if' scenarios. It's hindsight kicking into gear after you've made a decision that has unexpected consequences; it's everything while being on the emotional roller-coaster at the same time.

Despite what you may think, expect your professional advisors to always be pushing for the sale. Remember, they have a vested interest as they want to get paid and the sooner the better.

Fear and greed are sitting on both sides of the negotiation table—fear that the deal will fall through and fear that each side is spending money being at the negotiation table. Greed by the seller looking for a high valuation and number—greed by the potential buyers, as they want your business as it will add value to their business, and greed of the professional advisors, because they want to get paid and fear that they won't be if the deal falls through.

Expect the other side to be unreasonable. (When is your side ever unreasonable?!)

Expect to be told, 'The window is closing. We have to do this deal now.'

Expect the potential buyers to price chip. (Try and avoid this if it happens, by having an anti-price chipping agreement up-front.)

Expect your potential buyer to say, 'This is the set format we use to evaluate your business as it is how we acquire businesses.' That's utter rubbish, and all corporate organisations are bound to say this at the outset and throughout the negotiation process.

Be prepared for personality clashes, and even if the sale process is difficult, never burn your bridges.

Be prepared for the sale to fall through. It happens. Never count your chickens until they are hatched, and in this case, it's when the cash is in the bank, in your account.

What you will find is that time during the process will pass by very quickly, and there will be so many things going on that I strongly recommend you keep a timeline of key dates and a quick sentence on what happened. A diary would be ideal with frequent entries, but you may be short of time.

Three Golden Rules

Here are three golden rules worth remembering, and I would suggest plastering it on your bathroom mirror, in your wallet and anywhere else so you don't forget:

1. No manner how much planning and preparation you have done, expect the unexpected, because it will happen—guaranteed.
2. Before making a decision, check your emotions and make sure the decision is a logical one.
3. The deal isn't done until *all* the cash is in *your* bank account.

A Final Word in Closing

If you've exited the business, you may have planned your next venture, and already started it. Good luck to you! I hope you'll read this book again when you make the decision to sell that business. In the meantime, welcome to the exclusive club of business owners who have successfully sold their business. That's quite a feat. Congratulations!!!

Handy Tips

I've collated all the tips from throughout the book here for a quick and handy reference.

TIP: To make sure you don't miss the boat, define the indicators to look out for, which show when the best time to sell is approaching. Make sure this is checked regularly, so have it as an agenda item at your board meetings.

TIP: Think of selling your business like selling a house. Before you sell a house, you remove clutter, put on a fresh coat of paint, fix anything broken, and make it look as desirable as possible.

TIP: If a buyer offers you an EBITA multiple which is x8 or higher, logic says that it's most probably too much of a good thing. And if the multiple is x8 revenue definitely don't fall for it as it's a feint!

Tip: Avoid deal fever! First of all, acknowledge that it exists. Realise that numbers will usually be reduced. Buyers will look for any reason to chip down the value, so it's best not to count your chickens until they've hatched.

TIP: MI reports can be done retrospectively back to the beginning of your financial year, so you can track trends going forward. If you can create them for the last three years, that would be ideal to track the historic trends.

TIP: If your business uses Microsoft software packages internally, make sure you have a Microsoft Action Pack (MAP) subscription, as you will save hundreds of pounds on dishing out software licence fee payments. MAP offers cost-effective savings for internal use of software licences such as MS Office and Windows operating systems.

TIP: Have contracts available electronically, as the potential buyers will want to see them, and make sure that they are signed!

TIP: Do not commence any new ventures that require large capital expenditure or expand into a new market overseas

TIP: Reward your sales people for signed contracts by adding a 'contract signed' multiplier or bonus to encourage the salesperson to get the contract signed quickly. Consider having a sliding scale to reward for quicker contract signing (higher in month 1, lower in month 2, lowest in month 3, no bonus if later).

TIP: Ask your marketing or admin person to print off every document that a client might see. This includes every web page, profile page,

brochure, invoice, and so forth. You can then lay everything out on the floor and immediately see if anything is inconsistent, old or no longer necessary.

TIP: Introduce a clean desk policy and use the good reason 'to make it easier for the cleaners to do their job.'

TIP: Make it a policy that whenever an employee comes to you with a problem that they must also come with a couple possible of solutions in mind. This will force them to start thinking about solutions rather than relying on you for the answers.

TIP: Time spent on preparing your business for sale is worthwhile, as it will reduce the risk of exposure

TIP: You can work out a two-tier fee structure for corporate financiers; have a more expensive price for successful completion and a cheaper one if not.

TIP: Negotiate long tail termination clauses with your corporate financer carefully, as a situation where you change corporate financiers may arise.

TIP: Find out from your corporate solicitor which brokers they have worked with before, as it may be advantageous to work with the same team members.

TIP: If you choose not to use a tax advisor, your solicitor should be able to obtain tax clearance for you.

TIP: When you interview your potential broker, ask them what challenges they see when looking at your business to sell.

TIP: I found a couple of hours a week on either a squash or tennis court was a great stress reliever and helped me re-energise.

Tip: Before you make any short-listing decisions, draw up a pro/con list of each indicative offer and sleep on it.

Tip: Publicly listed companies on stock market exchanges will always carry out due diligence, it is part of their duties to their shareholders.

Tip: Have your company file server structure any information in the same format as your data room. It will save countless numbers of hours when you have to update the data room.

TIP: Your new service contract will not cover the terms of your earn-out (if applicable) as the earn-out forms part of the SPA.

TIP: If a customer has recently left the business, don't burn any bridges. Instead, keep in touch with regular contact, as you will most likely be asked by the potential buyer for this type of customer reference too.

TIP: If your visitors have to sign in, ask the visitors to use a different and/or fake company name and only give their first name at reception. This protects you against your staff doing a LinkedIn search and finding out who the visitors really are! This also protects you from other potential buyers who may be visiting afterwards, as they will definitely look through the visitor record book for clues.

TIP: Make sure to check with your solicitor that these escrow funds are earning interest, which accrues to shareholders in their shareholding proportions.

About Joanna Miller

When Joanna and her business partner sold their company, they went around the sales cycle a total of five times, had ten potential buyers at different times, and had four indicative price offers—of which the highest price was five times more than the lowest price. They even had a deal killed one week before Completion Day! On the sixth attempt, the business sold for millions.

Attempting to sell a UK business six times taught Joanna a variety of invaluable, but very expensive, lessons. By the final sale, Joanna learned every technique imaginable on how to maximise profits and sell quickly. Avoid frustration, save money, and enjoy a smoother business sale journey by discovering the wisdom, techniques, and tips offered in this book.

About Sell Your Business

Sell Your Business was created to help business owners through the complicated start-to-finish process of selling a company. Throughout the website, information and articles available at **SellYourBuziness.biz,** books, templates, packs and other resources, the creators of Sell Your Business aim to help you:

- Gain techniques and tips on how to best maximise your profit personally
- Demystify the business sale process so you can be one step ahead of the buyer rather than behind
- Be prepared to handle the emotional journey
- To increase the likelihood you sell the first time through the sale process
- Ensure the sale process goes as quickly and smoothly as possible
- To understand your current valuation and how to best increase it
- To avoid 'price chipping' (the buyer reducing the offer price) and costly mistakes
- Escape an earn-out (having to stay on as an employee and hit targets after the sale)
- To ultimately create a successful exit strategy so you can start a new adventure, enjoy more time with loved ones, spend some of your hard-earned cash, and do all the things you've always want to do but never had the time

Sell Your Business – Online Offerings

Save time, reduce stress, and increase your ability to maximise your business sale value today. Review our offerings and save money by purchasing one of our Collections. Purchase them securely from our online store now: **http://www.SellYourBusiness.biz/store**

'Preparation for Sale' Individual Offerings

The book **"How To Sell A Business: The #1 guide to maximising your company value and achieving a quick business sale"** will help you to get the highest pay-out, ensure a quick and smooth sale process, demystify the sale process, handle the emotional journey, and much more.

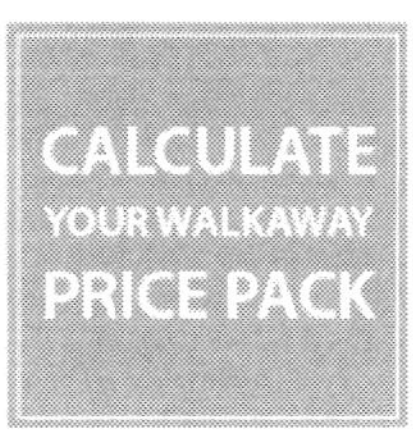

The **"Calculate Your Walkaway Price Pack"** is a step-by-step workbook that will enable you to calculate your minimum cash reward for selling your business.

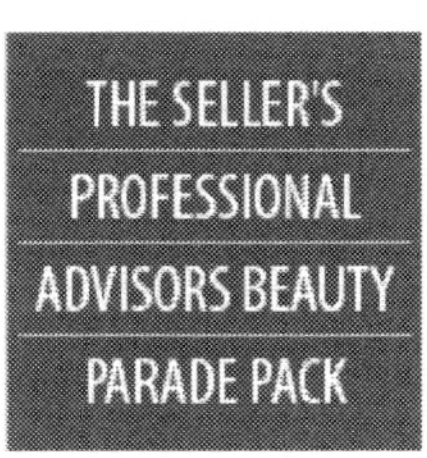

"The Seller's Professional Advisors Beauty Parade Pack" will help you find, interview and select the various professionals that will make up your final business sale success team. The pack will help you step-by-step with checklists, templates and lists of questions to ask so that no stone remains unturned!

'Preparation for Sale' Individual Offerings

The **"Contracts Summary Template"** is an Excel spreadsheet that will help you to record all your client contract information in one place. Use this timesaving template to organise your contracts, revenue and take action accordingly. Eliminate expirations, instigate renewals & monitor contracts.

The **"Monthly Management Information Report Template"** is an Excel spreadsheet that will allow you to easily organise your business' mission critical figures. Once populated, it will enable you to provide historical records of the business's progress helping you better plan and forecast.

'The Sale Journey' Individual Offerings

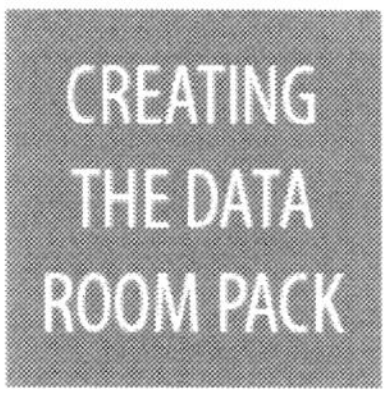

The **"Creating The Data Room Pack"** is for you if you want to make your life easier. To avoid running your company ***and*** frantically preparing all the data necessary for the buyers due diligence requests, be proactive and prepare get your data room set up now! Included is core information and file structure.

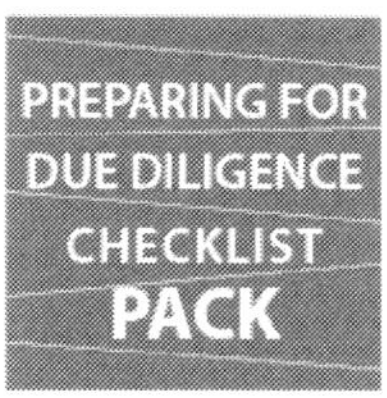

The **"Preparing For Due Diligence Checklist Pack"** comes after you set up your data room and provides you with the core documents, questions, requirements that will be requested. Be proactive and get this out of the way now rather than later.

The **"Due Diligence Questions Pack 1"** is similar to doing a practice run before an exam. The 250 questions will help you to be prepared for many of the requests that will be made by potential buyers during due diligence (DD) process. Free up time to allow you and your business sale team to focus on the negotiations and keeping the business value up.

'The Sale Journey' Individual Offerings

The **"Due Diligence Questions Pack 2"** offers 250 *more* questions that might be asked during the due diligence stage. If you want to cross every 't' and dot every 'i' this offering will help you do so! Proactively use your time now wisely - the more you prepare now the easier the process will flow.

"The Seller's Completion Day Checklist Pack" will help you to prepare yourself mentally and physically for Completion Day. If you want to reduce your stress levels, remove unknowns, prepare a negotiation strategy, and increase your chances for a successful completion get this pack now.

Money Saving Collections

The 'Ultimate Collection' consists of all offerings – Books, Templates, and Packs – everything! It will provide you with everything needed to help you prepare, increase your company value, help you avoid problem areas, save time and money and ensure your business sale process is as smooth and successful as possible.

The 'Everything But The Book Collection' is exactly what it says! Consider this money-saving offering if you already have the book and want to take advantage of all the templates, checklists and packs.

Purchase any of our items securely from our online store now:

http://www.SellYourBusiness.biz

Sell Your Business – Other Offerings

Please make sure to sign up to our weekly newsletter that will notify you of our recently published articles. Each week we send out information for people thinking of selling, preparing to sell and going through the sale process. Sign up here: http://www.SellYourBusiness.biz/broadcast/

Also check out our freebie section where we have the a number of samples including: Memorandum of Information table of contents, Business Sale Non-Disclosure Agreement, Teaser letter, Data room structure sample:

http://www.SellYourBusiness.biz/resources/free-document-samples/

23377677R00081

Printed in Great Britain
by Amazon